MODERN BUD[...]

BUDDHIST
CHANTS
& PRAYERS
FOR DAILY LIVING

MODERN BUDDHIST HEALING

———— ✳ ————

BUDDHIST CHANTS & PRAYERS
FOR DAILY LIVING

CHARLES ATKINS

JAICO PUBLISHING HOUSE

Mumbai Delhi Bangalore Kolkata
Hyderabad Chennai Ahmedabad Bhopal

Butala Emporium, New York

Tel : (718) 899-5590
Online @ www.indousplaza.com
Email : service@indousplaza.com

Published in arrangement with
Nicolas-Hays, Inc.
Berwick, Maine, USA

BUDDHIST CHANTS & PRAYERS FOR DAILY LIVING
ISBN 81-7992-437-8

First Jaico Impression: 2005
Third Jaico Impression: 2007

Printed by
Shri Krishna Printer
C-185-A, Hosiery Complex
Noida Phase II, Noida.

For my daughter Devin,
who inspired me to fight on,
when all seemed lost.

This book is also dedicated to the memory
of Nicolas-Hays publisher, visionary, and friend,
Betty Lundsted, 1941-2001.

Contents

CONTENTS

Acknowledgments

Many people have helped me tremendously in the process of writing this book. My gratitude to them is without limit. I would like to express my deepest appreciation for their advice, opinions, occasional scolding, encouragement, and heart-felt prayers. I would like to specifically thank the following people. I apologize if I have missed some names:

I thank my parents who gave me life and trained me to be strong, no matter what, and my grandparents, who gave me love, a sense of honor, and confidence. I thank Lynn Jacobs for her strength and enlightenment; Kathy Aitken of the UK for her sound editorial advice; Bill and Carolyn Thompson for urging me to write this book; Tom Friese for his friendship and pene-trating insight into the true aspect of prayer; Devin Atkins for her courageous faith, greatness, and healing prayers; Jennifer DuBois Atkins for her inspiration, support, and advice; Tom Filip, for his friendship, belief, and timely humor; Oncologist, Dr. William

Shulz, for his world-class medical skill; Hiromu Yamaguchi for his wisdom, expertise, and unrivaled professionalism; Celine Shinbutsu for her critical analysis, expert advice, and boundless expectations for this book; SGI friends, Frank Shimizu, Shoji Mita, Chizuko Edgington, Tomoko Sato, and Barbara Bates for their unwavering support, strict guidance, and powerful prayers during my darkest days; the SGI-USA publications staff for their many efforts to get my experience published; and all my beloved fellow Bodhisattvas of the Earth in the Soka Gakkai International.

I deeply thank the capable and caring staff who aided in my recovery at Hines Veterans Medical Center and Loyola University Medical Center in Maywood, Illinois. I deeply thank SGI Vice President Takehisa Tsuji for showing me how to save my life with prayer by first revealing what I respectfully call the "Tsuji Method" of chanting and visualization detailed in this book. Most of all, I wish to thank my Buddhist mentor in life, SGI President, Daisaku Ikeda, without whose vital encouragement and inspiration I would never have survived. This eternal, unbreakable bond with Daisaku Ikeda made this book possible.

Introduction

Not long ago, I learned that a young man named Corey was critically ill. One day he was healthy, the next day he was bedridden. The doctors were perplexed and had difficulty making an accurate diagnosis. My old friend Tom asked me to chant for Corey. A few years earlier, Tom had approached me for help when his own young son, Adams, was diagnosed with leukemia. I sent Adams instructions on how to chant and use visualization to combat his illness. I wrote him letters and encouraged him by phone. Most of all, I prayed for the best possible result. Adams got well.

I was in a quandary, because Corey's family had not asked me to help. Praying specifically for someone without their knowledge or permission is not always ethical. I felt that I should pray for and teach others about overcoming illness only when they directly asked me to do so. I always pray for the most positive result. Since 1987, either directly, or through my writings about

Buddhist healing, I had helped hundreds of people who were facing serious illness, but I had never faced such a confounding situation as this.

I struggled with this dilemma for a few days, and then received word that Corey had finally been diagnosed with advanced non-Hodgkin's lymphoma and had taken a rapid turn for the worse. The next day, I drove 150 miles to Chicago to see him face-to-face, even though I was a complete stranger. Ten minutes before I arrived, Corey died.

Corey's death drove home the importance of publishing a book on Buddhist healing. It is my experience that people desperately want a simple means to fight illness with their mind and spirit. People want a way to help their loved ones or friends who are facing a health crisis. After I had overcome advanced Hodgkin's lymphoma in 1987, which included a mind-blowing near-death experience, I painstakingly researched the compendium of writings on alternative healing and Western medicine. Doing so was an enormous but passionate challenge for me. I knew that each area that I studied deserved a lifetime of research, but I settled on being thorough and obtaining a basic grasp of the subjects. That process of study led me to Tibetan Medicine, Traditional Chinese Medicine, Qigong, Ayurveda, yoga, Christian faith healing, Buddhism, prayer therapy, guided imagery, and the cutting-edge philosophies of such innovators as Herbert Benson, Deepak Chopra, Norman Cousins, Larry Dossey, and Carl Jung.

I was raised as a Lutheran and became a Buddhist in 1974. In that time, I developed a healthy respect for the beliefs of others, and especially for the sacred teachings of the world's religions. In my role as a messenger of modern Buddhist healing who emerged from a Christian upbringing, it has been difficult for me to comprehend why certain theist factions would damn non-believers or spiritually inquisitive people. Fear and faith seem incompatible to me. I merely seek the truth of existence in a world full of strife, inexplicable randomness, and paradox. When cancer struck me at age thirty-six, I learned that no one has a monopoly on the truth; there is something important to learn and cherish from all traditions. Chanting *Nam-myoho-renge-kyo* to overcome illness is nonsectarian.

As a professional writer, I published many articles about my experience and findings, culminating in the presentation of an academic paper and lecture on Modern Buddhist Healing at the Socially Engaged Buddhism and Christianity Conference, held in 1996, at DePaul University in Chicago. The day before I presented my findings on chanting and visualization, my father died unexpectedly of a heart attack. It seemed like the universe had punctuated the moment. Although I was stunned, I felt it was imperative to present the paper and go on with the lecture. The result of that effort was the seed for this book.

In order for chanting and visualization to work, you do not need to understand Buddhism or alternative medicine any more than you need to understand the complexities of engine design in order to drive a car. Prayer and meditation are elegantly simple in nature, and are absolutely free. Prayer is our direct communication link to the absolute reality of life and the universe. The essence of Buddhist healing is simple enough for a child to master in a few moments and profound enough to humble a skilled physician.

My aim is to help those who are sick and suffering to empower themselves, especially when there is little or no hope. Having been there myself, I know how difficult overcoming a major health problem can be. Fortunately, when I was facing the ravages of cancer and death, I already knew the secret to victory over illness and suffering. To extend my own life, I tapped into that utterly impervious aspect of consciousness that is within us all. This grand state of being is completely free from the agonies of fear, pain, or death. All may enter with a prayer; no one is denied access.

We will explore how many people have overcome chronic, psychosomatic, and organic illness through their use of the essence of the *Lotus Sutra*, as taught by the Japanese Buddhist master, Nichiren. Although my viewpoint is Buddhist, the message is applicable to all people. In my research, it was obvious that physical and psychological healing is not the exclusive domain of any one religion or methodology, including cutting-edge allopathic techniques of somatic medicine. Genuine healing through faith has been evident in all cultures and spiritual traditions since the beginning of recorded history. What separates healing based on the essence of the *Lotus Sutra* from other forms of healing is the scope of its power to positively transform incredibly difficult situations.

After I recovered from my illness, I was determined that no one else should ever have to face illness or death without an effective mind-spirit defense and the means to make peace with the absolute reality. My intention is to share with you the Mystic Law of life and death. It is my sincere hope you will experience great benefit, good health, and eternal happiness.

In my description of Buddhist healing, you will not be asked to look outside yourself to God or gods, saviors, intermediaries, saints, or priests for results. I will merely ask you to look inside yourself with an open mind, and summon forth the courage to take a new and exciting action for your future.

PART ONE

THE
HEALING
STRATEGY

CHAPTER 1

Empowerment

Empowerment of the human spirit is at the core of Buddhist healing. When judging the validity of a spiritual teaching, actual proof is superior to theoretical or documentary proof. If something works for your health and happiness, and isn't negative or harmful, you're likely to use it. Being fully informed on what you are doing is the wisest course of action. Therefore, the most important message I can convey to you is: get the best medical treatment available. Proper diagnosis from a qualified physician is the first and foremost step in recovery.

The human body is more than a machine and it is more than an energy center. There is always a fundamental reason why illness appears; it has a physical aspect and a spiritual root. How does one eradicate the cause of illness? Western medicine attributes illness to physical realities. Eastern medicine looks at life energy, conduct, diet, and the mind. Merging these two diverse approaches seems to be the future of medicine. But no "physical" medicine, neither Western nor Eastern, can transform the fundamental cause that produced the illness in the first place. For that cure, we must go into the realm of faith, prayer, consciousness, and karma.

THE ORIGINS OF BUDDHIST HEALING

What I present here has its origins in the *Lotus Sutra* taught by Shakyamuni Buddha, more than 2,500 years ago in India. The essence of the *Lotus Sutra* was further advanced by the 13th-century Japanese Buddhist master, Nichiren Daishonin (1222–1282).

From the time of Shakyamuni Buddha to our modern era, healing by faith and spiritual practice has flourished throughout Asia and the world. Mahayana Buddhism teaches that all people are originally enlightened and fully-endowed with the latent potential to heal themselves. In many cases, Western medical science is now actively using Buddhist meditation techniques like visualization as part of cancer therapy. What is Buddhist healing? What are the principles that explain its reality? How can a person of any belief use Buddhist chanting and visualization to advance against their illness? The Buddha's *Lotus Sutra* contains powerful medicine for the illness of all people. That medicine is the mantra *Nam-myoho-renge-kyo*. Pain, suffering, sickness, and death are the realities that we all must face at some point. We seek to extend our lives and overcome our fear of dying.

THE BUDDHA

Shakyamuni, also known as Siddhartha or Gautama, was the historical first Buddha. According to the Pali Canon (the earliest of the Buddhist texts), he was born to the Shakya lineage of Nepal, about 2500 years ago, as Prince Siddhartha. When he became aware of the suffering outside his palace walls, he renounced his royal heritage and pursued the spiritual life. His goal was to solve the four dire obstacles, or "Four Sufferings," that all human beings face: birth, old age, sickness, and death. In spreading his teachings, or dharma, through a multitude of sutras over a period of fifty years, Buddha taught according to the capacity of the people, using expedient means of teaching such as similes, metaphors, parables, meditation, diet, and breath control. The Buddha's dharma includes rules of conduct to guide people to a correct way of living, a way in which people could improve their karma and reach a state of enlightenment, or *nirvana*.

In the final eight years of Buddha's life, he preached the *Lotus Sutra*, which he designated as his highest teaching and reason for his advent. He told his followers that all of his preceding teachings were expedient means, and not the entire truth of his message. He stipulated that there were not two or three vehicles to enlightenment, just One Great Vehicle known as the *Lotus Sutra*. He declared that all people had the Buddha nature within them, including women. Buddha's acknowledgment of women as equal to men and originally enlightened was more than two millennia ahead of its time.

In the more than twenty-five hundred years since Shakyamuni's death, various sects and schools of Buddhism have

utilized pre-*Lotus Sutra* teachings, mantras, mudras, yoga postures, breath control practices, meditative disciplines, and various rituals to effectuate healing in the body, mind, and spirit of
believers.

KARMA

Buddhism is like a science of life that examines the causes of suffering and happiness. It categorizes and clearly identifies the
causes of sickness, as well as provides various remedies for
changing the problem. What we think, say, and do determine the
consequences of our future, for better or worse. Our lot in life
and the sum total of our thoughts, speech, and actions are known
as *karma*, a Sanskrit word meaning "action."

When we are born into this world, there is a wide disparity
of fortune from one child to the next. In the early 1950s, when
polio was afflicting so many children, I happened to visit with a
boy who was in an iron lung. I wondered why he suffered so
much and I suffered so little. His situation troubled me very
much, because I couldn't comprehend why God would have
some children suffer while others did not. Where did that destiny
come from? It wasn't until I discovered Eastern philosophy that
I pieced together the puzzle of destiny.

When illness strikes, often there seems to be no continuity
between a person's actions and what has happened. It seems as if
they had been randomly chosen to suffer. When no reason for the
unexpected suffering is apparent, the bad fortune is often
ascribed to "God's Will." I clearly recall a case when I was a teen
and our neighbor died of breast cancer, leaving behind five children and a devoted husband. When I asked my pastor about it,

he said that God's Will is often difficult to understand. No doubt. But that was not the only time I was faced with the explanation that the misfortune of illness, accident, or tragedy was God's Will. It seems to me that the proper definition of God's Will is actually karma.

CONSCIOUSNESS

Mahayana Buddhism identifies nine levels of consciousness associated with all life. The first six are: the five senses of taste, touch, smell, sound, sight, and the conscious mind. On a basic level, the seventh realm is the *manos-vijnana*—the subconscious, where all bodily functions are managed, and from whence the impulses for survival emerge. The manos consciousness is the integrator and processor of all sensory input.

The eighth level is what the psychologist Carl Jung termed "the collective unconscious." In Mahayana Buddhism, it is called the *alaya-vijnana*, or karma repository. Alaya consciousness is the limitless storehouse of perceptions, conceptions, words, and actions that we experience or create in life. At the same time, the eighth level is an ethereal seed bank of our latent karma, which we experience in life as we interact with our environment. Alaya-vijnana has its counterparts in countless other modern and ancient traditions: Deepak Chopra's quantum consciousness; Larry Dossey's concept of non-local consciousness; the Akashic Record; the bardo states of intermediate existence after manifest life. They are all the same thing—a sort of "on-ramp" to the ultimate reality, the actual source of healing and the ninth level of consciousness known as *amala-vijnana* in Mahayana Buddhism.

Amala-vijnana, or cosmic consciousness, is the true entity of life, fundamentally pure, and impervious to time, space, suffering, or death. The karmic seed bank of aiaya-vijnana and the cosmic consciousness amala-vijnana fuse with the universe at death, to be reborn, reassembling themselves as a living being comprised of the five components of form, perception, conception, volition, and consciousness.

Buddhism teaches that there is no such thing as pure matter or pure spirit; there is only the ultimate reality of life itself, which invariably manifests both a physical and spiritual aspect, no matter how coarse or fine the actual manifestation. This ultimate, unchanging reality flows through both the physical and spiritual, in an ever-changing cycle of actualization and dormancy. For this reason, the Western idea of an individual soul does not exist in Buddhism. The Buddhist view sees our individual incarnations as ephemeral unions of form, perception, conception, volition, and consciousness, all of which merges into pure consciousness when we die, like moisture returning to the sea. In Christianity the idea of an individual soul is central to the idea of life after death in heaven. If there is no soul, as Buddhism asserts, then what is that spiritual essence of ours that journeys into the afterlife? If there is no eternal soul or self, what is there? The thought of annihilation of personal consciousness is troubling indeed, unless you understand that the true entity of your life *is life,* as vast as the universe, indestructible, and eternal.

At the root of karma is the eternity of life. Virtually every religion teaches that life is eternal, although they differ on the conditions. I was taught that life begins as an original soul that, after death, lives forever. In Buddhism, there is no discontinuity between the past, present, and future. If the fundamental cause for illness is not apparent or the illness is inherited, we might consider the eternity of life and the causes we brought forward to this existence. We often think that "the eternity of life" means that after we die, we each live forever as a soul in heaven. That's what I was taught. Actually, eternity means *without beginning or end*.

Contemplating eternity staggers the mind, especially when we consider the idea that each life has no beginning; it has always existed, repeating the two states of life and death in an unbroken pattern. If we have lived before, not once or twice, but countless times, it would help explain why there is so much suffering in the world and the seemingly inexplicable randomness of it all.

Even acknowledging that we may have lived before still does not answer the question of what kind of karmic causes we made for us to experience life as we do, because we can't see back into our previous lives. Many of us can't even remember the details of our childhood or the faces of friends we haven't seen in twenty years. Even if we could know with certainty what we did in our previous lives, what could we actually do about it that would solve our problems today? Changing karma in the alaya-vijnana is a function of *Nam-myoho-renge-kyo* and is the means by which even diseases such as advanced cancer can possibly be overcome.

KARMA AND THE CAUSES OF ILLNESS

Karma has often been associated with guilt and negativity. Karma is actually regarded as neutral in that free will can change something negative into something positive or vice-versa; it depends what we do with the circumstance. Many of the famous advocates of self-healing seem to have distanced themselves from the pre-Buddhist principle of karma and individual accountability as if it were some baseless holdover of medieval superstition. Regarding illness and the judgment of God(s), or what Buddhists might term "negative" karma, John Camp described this conundrum in his book, *Magic, Myth and Medicine:* "The idea that illness and disease were brought about by the displeasure of the gods has meant that the art of healing has always been closely linked with religious beliefs. Such beliefs did not always help medical progress, for as religious thought became more organized, and a single God displaced the many gods of ancient times, the rights and wrongs of man-made healing became a major issue.[1]

Buddha taught that negative karma can and does manifest as illness of the body, mind, and spirit. The seemingly incomprehensible, interdependent cause and effect relationship of thoughts, words, and deeds carried over from one lifetime to the next, manifesting as affliction and circumstance, has not been embraced by many of the popular advocates of self-healing. Nichiren addressed the subject of karma and illness in his *Gosho* ("honored writings," used to refer to the body or an individual piece of Nichiren's writing), "On Curing Karmic Illness":

The Nirvana Sutra reads: "There are three types of people whose illness is extremely difficult to cure. The first is those who slander the great vehicle; the second, those who commit the five cardinal sins; and the third, *iccha-*

---

[1] John Michael Francis Camp, *Magic, Myth & Medicine* (New York: Taplinger, 1974), p. 105.

ntikas, or persons of incorrigible disbelief. These three categories of illness are the gravest in the world."

It also states: "One who creates evil karma in this life . . . will surely suffer in hell. . . . But by making offerings to the three treasures [Samgha], one can avoid falling in hell and instead receives retribution in this life, in the form of afflictions of the head, eye, or back." *Great Concentration and Insight* [the *Maka Shikan*] states, "Even if one has committed grave offenses . . . their retribution can be lessened in this life. Thus, illness occurs when evil karma is about to be dissipated."[2]

Buddhism reveals that the reality of life is shaped by karmic cause and effect in an unbroken pattern from the infinite past. In relationship to illness and healing, the Chinese Buddhist master Chih-i, founder of the Tendai School of Buddhism, delineated six causes of illness.

The first cause of illness is disorders of the five elements of the human body: earth, wind, fire, water, and *ku*. Earth is the flesh, wind is our respiration, fire is our metabolism, water is the blood and fluids of our body, and *ku* (or *shunyata*) is the spiritual potential of life and consciousness that transcends existence and non-existence. The second cause is immoderate eating and drinking. The third cause is improper practice of seated meditation, but has also been designated as a life out of rhythm with itself and the world. The fourth is an attack by external forces that the ancients called demons, but in modern terms we call

---

[2] Nichiren Daishonin, *The Writings of Nichiren Daishonin* (Tokyo: Soka Gakkai, 1999), p. 631.

pathogens, disease germs, or environmental poisons. The fifth cause is termed the "work of devils." These are latent, internal conditions that emerge when the time or circumstances are right. The fifth type of illness might include a genetic predisposition or emergence of chemical imbalances, or diseases such as cancer, diabetes, or heart disease. The sixth cause is the effects of karma that often appear without a direct causal link to any misconduct in one's present life. The first four causes manifest as physical illness, and the fifth and sixth causes of illness manifest as both physical and mental illness. When we understand that karma is the law of cause and effect operating on the physical and spiritual levels, we can see all illness as actually being the result of karma. To change karma that is unresponsive to any treatment requires the power of *Nam-myoho-renge-kyo*. But if we are to avoid making the causes that create illness, we must first understand what to avoid.

What creates bad karma has been spelled out by the major religions of the world. Buddhism has laid down "ten evil acts" that result in negative karma and cause one to be reborn into the Four Evil Paths—Hell, Hunger, Animality, and Anger. There are three physical acts of killing, stealing, and sexual misconduct. The four verbal acts are lying, flattery or irresponsible speech, defamation, and duplicity. The three mental evils arise from holding mistaken views and are known as greed, anger, and stupidity. Those basic ten evil acts have numerous shadings that include betrayal, cheating, intentionally harming others, and so on. These actions create karmic debt that must be paid back later; some effects appear immediately and others show up in later rebirths. With karma, nothing is ever missed, no virtuous act unrewarded, or evil deed unreturned.

12

From a modern perspective, contributing factors to creating our own future health problems might include such attitudes and behaviors as: complaint, cynicism, criticism, rage, cruelty, vanity, vindictiveness, perversity, ruthlessness, addiction, sorrow, apathy, and having no passionate life work.

Slander is an extremely negative cause that results in the most severe effects, including incurable illness manifesting in a single lifetime or appearing in an indeterminate number of subsequent existences. Slander arises in fourteen different ways, through: arrogance; negligence; arbitrary, egotistical judgment; shallow, self-satisfied understanding; attachment to earthly desires; lack of a seeking spirit; not believing; aversion; deluded doubt; vilification; contempt; hatred; jealousy; and holding grudges.

Obviously, we humans are in many ways products of our environment and upbringing. The events of life often hammer us down like protruding nails. It is hard to live up to the examples of moral conduct, attitude, and conviction that the past masters have shown us. Yet it is our thoughts, words, and deeds that constitute our current state and will determine our future. For this reason, having the intent to improve our ways is the most important step of all.

MEDITATION

Dhyana is a Sanskrit word that means "meditation." It is generally a practice of focusing the mind on one point to purify the heart, dissolve illusion, and realize truth. From the discipline of dhyana, Zen Buddhism rose out of China, purporting meditation as the sole means of attaining enlightenment. Practiced even before the time of Shakyamuni, dhyana was an integral practice in eradicating illusion and perceiving truth. Dhyana in Buddhism is the fulfillment of the fifth of the six *paramitas* (practices to attain enlightenment—see Glossary). But meditation is not such a simple concept as closing the eyes and stilling the mind.

Dhyana includes the constant practice of four ascending levels of meditation that result in self-mastery and the promise of favorable spiritual rebirth. Under the direction of a mentor, one undergoes a varied and complex series of exercises and lifestyle constraints that can take the form of diet restrictions, mudras, mantras, yoga, esoteric meditations, and mandala meditations. From this way of life, which cannot be fully achieved in a casual manner, one seeks to gain knowledge, wisdom, spiritual power, and enlightenment. Upon completion of the first stage of dhyana, the meditator is freed of desires arising from their senses, as well as from their past evil deeds. This supposedly produces feelings of boundless pleasure, but to move deeper into the stages of dhyana, even pleasure must be transcended. But consider the idea that mastering just the first stage of meditation might not be possible during a single lifetime. It was once believed that the paramita of meditation took many thousands of lifetimes to achieve.

Dhyana's second level results in razor-sharp mental powers of a transcendental quality and experiencing true inner serenity. The third level brings feelings of unbridled joy, composure, and firmness of mind. The fourth level produces a mental and spiritual state that transcends both joy and suffering.

The second major type of meditation is called *samadhi,* which involves intensely focusing and concentrating the mind on one point without letting it waver, which produces a state of inner serenity. Samadhi states of consciousness are described in the *Lotus Sutra* and are ever ascending, eventually leading to supreme and perfect enlightenment. All schools of meditation and spiritual prayer can be classified in the two categories of dhyana and samadhi. For example, when a Christian looks at the cross and prays or meditates, they are practicing samadhi, while a Quaker in contemplative silence might be considered practicing the first level of dhyana. Nichiren Daishonin taught that meditation or samadhi means chanting *Nam-myoho-renge-kyo*.

BODY & MIND

When we are sick, we expect our physician to prescribe the most effective medicine so we can get well as soon as possible. We trust our physician to make the right diagnosis and administer the proper treatment. We should ask no less for our mind and spirit. There is a mirror image relationship between our body and mind. Although body and mind seem to be two, they are actually inseparable, like the two sides of a coin. In Buddhism, this ancient principle is termed *shiki-shin funi*. Conventional medicine is good at fixing the body when it malfunctions, but what of the mind and spirit? Psychosomatic illness is a scientific fact, and so is the beneficial effect of prayer and faith on the immune system. The importance in the oneness of body and mind in our quest for recovery is knowing how to influence the reciprocal nature of our body and mind, like simply pushing a button to calibrate a sensitive instrument.

The principle of the oneness of body and mind, *shiki-shin funi*, is one of the most compelling concepts in Buddhist healing.

More accurately, shiki-shin funi is the essential oneness of the material and spiritual. Modern science has opened new paths in psychosomatic medicine and is rapidly approaching the ancient wisdom that the mind and body are two, yet not two. Body and mind, or spirit, are inseparably linked, exerting reciprocal influence on each other. Further, the body is not the basis for the mind and vice versa.

In interpreting the relationship between body and mind in terms of the true entity of all phenomena, the Buddhist teacher T'ien-t'ai regards the distinction between material and spiritual as pertaining to the level of "all phenomena," and their essential oneness, to that of "true entity."[3] The oneness of body and mind, or of matter and spirit, is an expression of the true entity or ultimate reality of life. Nichiren Daishonin states in the "Record of Orally Transmitted Teachings," the "Ongi Kuden": "The ultimate principle reveals that these two [the physical and the spiritual] are integral aspects of every single life."[4]

When the mind is disturbed, there is a corresponding depression in the immune system, whereas faith, happiness, and encouragement seem to bolster the immune system. The integrating force of the oneness of body and mind is the life-dynamic of Nam-myoho-renge-kyo. This knowledge and power is especially valuable for children stricken by cancer and debilitating disease, as well as for their parents, because chanting offers tremendous hope for the innocent and it is easy for them to master.

---

[3] The writings of T'ien-t'ai appear in *The Taisho Shinshu Daizokyo* published by The Society for the Publication of the Tripitaka, 1924-1934, Japan. They are in Chinese and, to my knowledge, only fragments have been translated into English.
[4] Nichiren Daishonin, *Gosho Zenshu* (Tokyo: Soka Gakkai, 1952), p. 708.

The mind is always in a radical state of flux in relationship with the external world and therefore cannot be completely relied on to bring forth healing. Therefore, the reality of attaining a true harmonious body-mind relationship is not possible until we recognize and employ a third, much deeper source of healing. This spiritual force has many different names all over the world, including: the Holy Spirit, *prana*, *chi*, *kundalini*, and life force. Throughout history, spiritual masters have looked to God in order to understand our life in the universe, while contemporary physicists have sought the same knowledge of a unifying law that encompasses the quantum world with the macrocosm. Even before the days of Moses, holy men asserted that God's name was unknowable and inexpressible; only in death was such grace possible. Today, scientists study the cosmos, superluminal phenomena, light waves, and such mysterious subatomic particles as tachyons, luxons, and neutrinos in search of that ultimate unifying principle. Nichiren revealed this Mystic Law or absolute reality as *Nam-myoho-renge-kyo*.

NICHIREN AND THE DAIMOKU
OF THE LOTUS SUTRA

Time has proven that Nichiren Daishonin (1222-1282) was an unrivaled Buddhist master. Describing Nichiren, the late British historian, Arnold Toynbee wrote: "'Prophet' is an appropriate description of Nichiren; for in many ways Nichiren has more affinity with the prophets of Western Asia than with any of the other propagators and interpreters of Buddhism in India and in Eastern Asia. Zoroastrian, Muslim, Christian, and Jewish readers will recognize Nichiren's affinity with Zarathustra, Muhammad, and the prophets of Israel and Judah."[5]

Nichiren gave birth to the widespread chanting of the *Lotus Sutra*'s title and essence, *Nam-myoho-renge-kyo*, stating that this was the supreme medicine for all illnesses of body, mind, and spirit. What does *Nam-myoho-renge-kyo* mean? It expresses the true entity of life that allows each individual to directly tap his or her enlightened nature. Only its invocation can reveal its deepest meaning, but the literal meaning of *Nam-myoho-renge-kyo* is: devotion, the fusion of one's life with the universal (*Nam*); the entity of the universe and its phenomenal manifestations is the Mystic Law (*myoho*); the simultaneity of cause and effect (represented in the lotus, *renge*, which is the only known flower to bear seeds and blossom at the same time); and all phenomena and activities in life (*kyo*, Buddha's teaching).

Nichiren instructed his contemporary and future followers to chant *Nam-myoho-renge-kyo* (also referred to as "daimoku") and overcome all their obstacles based on faith in the mandala he inscribed, commonly known as the Gohonzon. The mandala created by Nichiren is not the traditional round configuration but a rectangular scroll. Inscribed down its center is the mantra "*Namu-myoho-renge-kyo*, Nichiren"; this is flanked by the names of the Buddhas Shakyamuni and Many Treasures, who are depicted in the eleventh chapter of the *Lotus Sutra*, "Emergence of the Treasure Tower." Included on the Gohonzon are the names of various Buddhist gods who represent the elemental functions of the universe, as well as the gamut of life conditions we all pos-

---

5 Cited in Daisaku Ikeda, "The One Essential Phrase Part 2," in *World Tribune*, June 7, 1996, p. 9.

sess, known as the Ten Worlds (see Glossary). Nichiren described the Gohonzon as the object of devotion for observing one's mind. By chanting *Nam-myoho-renge-kyo* while focusing your eyes and attention on the Gohonzon, Buddha consciousness can be attained and prayers realized.

Of the Gohonzon, Nichiren writes in his letter, "Reply to Kyo-o," "Believe in this mandala with all your heart. *Nam-myoho-renge-kyo* is like the roar of a lion. What sickness can therefore be an obstacle?"[6]

Nichiren implies that nothing is impossible with faith *and* prayer. This is a common theme in all religions. Faith without prayer is little more than wishful thinking. Prayer without faith is like work without joy, or marriage without love.

While Nichiren claimed that any illness could be overcome through strong faith and prayer, he also placed great importance on getting proper diagnosis and the best possible medical treatment. Never did he suggest that faith alone would enable a person to disregard treatment. He strongly encouraged a stubborn, elderly follower to take proper care of her illness: "If you are unwilling to make efforts to heal yourself, it will be very difficult to cure your illness. . . . In addition you can go to Shijo Kingo, who is not only an excellent physician, but a Votary of the *Lotus Sutra*."[7]

Drawing enlightenment and hope from the mighty ocean of the *Lotus Sutra*, Nichiren nourished his followers with the life-sustaining encouragement that by virtue of their faith and deter-

6 Nichiren Daishonin, *The Writings of Nichiren Daishonin*, p. 412.
7 Nichiren Daishonin, "On Prolonging One's Life Span," in *The Writings of Nichiren Daishonin*, p. 955.

mined practice they could overcome any illness, extend their life-span, die a victorious death, and be joined by a thousand Buddhas who would guide them to nirvana.

Buddhist practice redirects attention away from external gods or saviors to the latent potential of Buddhahood at the core of human life that each of us can activate through chanting. This realization that enlightenment exists inherently and is imbued with unlimited healing power is the *prima facie* cause that in the cancer patient promotes a dynamically energetic immune response as well as a more synchronized spirit-body relationship.

By using the correct meditation of chanting *Nam-myoho-renge-kyo*, we can arouse and make manifest the life condition of Buddhahood from within. The state of Buddhahood definitely exists in all life, originating beyond the alaya-vijnana, or what C. G. Jung termed the collective unconscious.

In regard to Buddhist healing, when we chant *Nam-myoho-renge-kyo*, we are calling on the Mystic Law with our spirit and mind to emerge like an equatorial sun from the depths of cosmic consciousness and to positively transform and nourish the karmic seeds in the eighth level of alaya-vijnana. Through this process, negative health karma is burned up once and for all, so that even if illness takes our life, we will be rid of that destiny in our next existence.

From the standpoint of modern healing, an increasing number of highly respected medical schools are teaching new doctors about alternative medicine, including meditation, yoga relaxation techniques, prayer therapy, and guided imagery. Is there a meditation, prayer, and system of imagery that can empower people and, at the same time, positively transform the original cause that brought forth illness in the first place? *Nam-myoho-renge-kyo* is that method of meditation, prayer, and imagery all rolled into one. I call this combination of prayer and visualization "mantra-powered visualization."

At the root of the Mystic Law is the boundless source of energy, consciousness, and synchronicity we call life. This vast power to heal and elevate consciousness already exists inside us. All we need do is tap into it and bring it out. We need no special skills or abilities to promote healing. Maintaining a state of equilibrium is the natural inclination of the body and mind. Buddhist healing goes directly to the cause of illness on a consciousness level. Shakyamuni declared in the 23rd chapter ("The Former Affairs of the Bodhisattva Medicine King") of the *Lotus Sutra*:

> Such is the *Lotus Sutra*. It can cause living beings to cast off all distress, all sickness and pain. It can unloose all the bonds of birth and death. . . . Among all sutras, it holds the highest place. And just as among all the stars and their like, the moon, a god's son, is foremost. So this *Lotus Sutra* is likewise. For among all the thousands, ten thousands, millions of types of sutra teachings, it shines the brightest. And just as the sun, a god's son, can banish all darkness, so too this sutra is capable of destroying the darkness of all that is not good.[8]

If someone is critically ill and they or their family prays to God or Jesus Christ for deliverance and are blessed with recovery, it

---

8 Burton Watson, tr., *The Lotus Sutra* (Columbia University Press, 1993), p. 286.

does not diminish or contradict the power of the *Lotus Sutra* to heal or pave the way for a peaceful, dignified death and fortunate rebirth. By the same token, chanting *Nam-myoho-renge-kyo* does not conflict with other religious practices. Buddhism clearly recognizes and respects the beauty, intrinsic value, history, and diversity of the world's myriad spiritual teachings. What's important is the removal of suffering from our lives, not whose mythology is most popular. Chanting daimoku raises the awesome power that metaphorically changes poison into medicine at the core of our being. Chanting cultivates happiness in our daily life, elevates our life condition from weakness or confusion into strength and clarity. It mystically causes benefits unique to our individual happiness to appear, and it enables us to muster the resolve to overcome our personal obstacles, no matter how daunting they may seem at the moment.

What is at work in the *Lotus Sutra* is far more than a bounty of beautiful metaphors, timeless legends, or rapturous, spiritual praise. The essence of the Buddha's message is that *Nam-myoho-renge-kyo* is the foremost spiritual medicine for people who are suffering and ill. The message of Buddha is that simple.

For nearly three decades, I have studied Nichiren's teachings in order to understand the nature of prayer and compassion as outlined in the *Lotus Sutra*. In the world of spirituality, it is a superior teaching. Nichiren left a legacy of personal letters and scholarly writings based on the *Lotus Sutra* that clarifies how to overcome illness and suffering through the practice of Buddhism. In his writing, "The Daimoku of the Lotus

---

9 Nichiren Daishonin, *The Writings of Nichiren Daishonin*, p. 149. Brackets are mine.

Sutra," he quotes the great teacher Miao-lo, who said, "Because [the *Lotus Sutra*] can cure that which is thought to be incurable, it is called *myo* or mystic."[9]

In another important work, "Reply to Ota Saemon-no-jo," Nichiren wrote: "The *Lotus Sutra* is beneficial medicine for all illnesses of body and mind. Therefore it states, 'This sutra is beneficial medicine for the illnesses of all mankind. If one is ill and can hear this sutra, his illness will vanish immediately, and he will find perpetual youth and eternal life.'"[10]

An extremely unusual trait seems to emerge when people chant *Nam-myoho-renge-kyo* that can be objectively seen by others as well as subjectively experienced. Instead of growing old in spirit, people who chant become youthful and enthusiastic. This transformation is most evident when an elderly or weakened person starts to chant. They invariably become vigorous and youthful in spirit as if they were in their twenties again, but enjoying the wisdom of experience. Few things are as taxing on people's psychological age or health as cynicism, apathy, depression, and having no mission or passion for the future. Nichiren wrote, "This Buddha expounded on the medicine of immortality. This is the five characters of *myoho-renge-kyo* we have today. Moreover, he specifically taught that these five characters are 'good medicine for the illnesses of all the people of Jambudvipa [the world].'"[11]

"The illnesses of all the people of the world" can be interpreted both literally and as a metaphor. Literally, it implies that

---

[10] Nichiren Daishonin, *Gosho Zenshu*, p. 1915.
[11] Nichiren Daishonin, "The Good Medicine for All Ills" in *The Writings of Nichiren Daishonin*, p. 937.

chanting will put us in touch with our true identity, enabling us to see the eternity of our lives, allay the nagging fears of death, and awaken our inner power to overcome illness and suffering. From a metaphorical standpoint it implies that chanting is the solution to the misdirection of people and society as a whole.

CHAPTER 2

Faith, Prayer, and
Their Modern Proponents

Despite numerous technical advances in Western medicine, many people have expressed serious doubts that pure physical science can cure our ills. That fact has in turn created a $13 billion a year alternative medicine industry. With the advent of AIDS and the continuing horror of incurable cancers, people have turned to body-mind and faith healing. In answer to the public's thirst for spiritual remedies and body-mind philosophy, certain contemporary seers have ʌmerged to redefine the role of the individual in their own healing. Thus an innovative group of physicians, now turned authors, have introduced us to the amazing powers and forgotten history of self-healing and our symbiotic relationship with the universe.

Harvard professor Dr. Herbert Benson conducted extensive studies on the effectiveness of faith and prayer in healing. He

termed the measurable influence of faith and prayer "the relaxation response," which he details in his book of the same title. He
determined that what he calls "the faith factor" in a patient's
prayer correlated to the degree that the patient's immune system
was stimulated. With the relaxation response induced by prayer,
patients were better able to reach a state of what Dr. Benson
termed "remembered wellness." The patient's faith is the key in
the healing process.

In his book *Timeless Healing: The Power and Biology of
Belief,* Dr. Benson confirmed, through clinical studies, the benefit of faith and prayer in eliciting the relaxation response and
leading patients to remembered wellness. The study concluded
that repetitive prayer, born of faith, is a highly effective adjunct
to conventional medical treatment. The essence of that clinical
study found measurable recuperative benefits were consistently
obtained by chronically ill Christians, Jews, and Muslims who
used repetitive prayer in conjunction with the best medical treatment available. Dr. Benson postulated that as long as the mantra
or prayer is personally affirmative, it induces healthful physical
changes such as lower blood pressure, better regulated heart
rates, and lower metabolic rates.

Dr. Benson indicated that the evidence points toward all
mantras, prayers, and secular affirmations being equal in producing the relaxation response. For example, a Jew chanting
"Shalom" or a Muslim reciting passages from the Koran would
experience the same benefits as a Hindu chanting "Om" or a
Christian repeating the 23rd Psalm. Even secular affirmations
such as "I will overcome, no matter what," produced the benefits of the relaxation response and remembered wellness.
Referring to how healing was accomplished in the past, Dr.

Benson wrote, "Because these superstitions and legends were accepted and touted by healers, they undoubtedly fostered remembered wellness. And up until a hundred years ago, remembered wellness was the treatment of choice."[1]

Norman Cousins wrote a number of pioneering books on self-healing such as *The Healing Heart: Antidotes to Panic and Helplessness; Head First: The Biology of Hope;* and *Anatomy of an Illness as Perceived by the Patient: Reflections on Healing and Regeneration.* Mr. Cousins was able to bring mind-body healing to the forefront of the public's attention, extolling the benefit of laughter and positive thinking in recovery.

In his book *Head First: Biology of Hope,* Mr. Cousins exposes five basic misconceptions that explain much about the mind-body relationship and that seem to dominate our thinking about health:

1. Almost all illnesses are caused by disease germs or other external factors.

2. Illness proceeds in a straight line unless interrupted by outside intervention in one form or another.

3. Pain is always a manifestation of disease and the elimination of pain is therefore a manifestation of a return to "good" health.

4. What goes into the mind has little or no effect on the body (and vice versa).

---

[1] Herbert Benson, M.D., with Marge Stark, *Timeless Healing: The Power and Biology of Belief* (New York: Scribner, 1996) p. 109.

5. Old age is connected to numbers, beginning at 65, at which
    point mental and physical abilities begin to fall off signifi-
    cantly, and therefore society is justified in mandating retire-
    ment based on age.[2]

*Superimmunity: Master Your Emotions and Improve Your
Health,* by Paul Pearsall, Ph.D., struck a powerful chord with
people who sought to bolster their immune system by understanding and controlling hot and cold emotions and the ever-
changing mind. Far ahead of his time, Dr. Pearsall recognized the
quantum nature of human life, health, and our relationship to
the universe. "Our immunity is enhanced when we learn that our
mechanistic, dualistic, simplistic thinking is not in keeping with
the laws of the universe."[3]

Author and cosmic philosopher Dr. Deepak Chopra has put
forward such ideas as quantum healing, realizing perfect health,
reversing the aging process, balancing the doshas (see Glossary)
of the human body, and the importance of humanity's accep-
tance of a quantum world-view. Dr. Chopra's emergence from
the constraints of conventional Western medicine spawned an
explosion of insight influenced largely by ancient Hindu
Ayurvedic medicine. Dr. Chopra's observations on life and consciousness as energy fields, and that we are integral components
of a universal, all-pervading intelligence are important ideas in
understanding the elements involved in self-healing. Quantum
consciousness breaks down matter into intelligent fields, waves,

---

[2] Norman Cousins, *Head First: The Biology of Hope and the Healing Power of
the Human Spirit* (New York: Dutton, 1989), p. 243.
[3] Paul Pearsall, *Superimmunity: Master Your Emotions and Improve Your
Health* (Boston: McGraw-Hill, 1987), p. 235.

and subatomic particles. Dr. Chopra's opinions have very important implications with regard to guided imagery when he writes, "Every cell is a little sentient being. Sitting in the liver or heart or kidney, it 'knows' everything you know, but in its own fashion."[4]

Larry Dossey, M.D. has written and spoken about prayer and self-healing in its varied forms and has introduced people to such Buddhist-like ideas as nonlocal consciousness, which transcends space-time, and our ability to initiate recovery through prayer. His book *Healing Words: The Power of Prayer and the Practice of Medicine* affirms what millions of people already know and believe—that prayer could make possible the impossible. Dr. Dossey has done extensive research in virtually hopeless situations where ordinary medical intervention failed but prayer seemed to work; in time-displaced prayer; negative prayer effect; prayer involving dreams; and telesomatic events. His book *Prayer is Good Medicine: How to Reap the Healing Benefits of Prayer* further explores his premise that prayer has always been medicine's best-kept secret. In his best-seller *Healing Words*, Dr. Dossey offers an intriguing perspective on the true nature of our prayers for recovery, the transient nature of illness, the eternity of life, and the transcendental essence of the fundamentally enlightened human spirit: "Even if prayer or attempts at self-transformation fail in the course of illness, there is still a sense in which a cure can always occur. By "cure" I do not mean the *physical* disappearance of cancer, heart disease, high blood pressure, or stroke, but something more marvelous—the realization that

---

[4] Deepak Chopra, *Quantum Healing: Exploring the Frontiers of Mind/Body Medicine* (New York: Bantam, 1990), p. 146.

physical illness, no matter how painful or grotesque, is at some level of secondary importance in the total scheme of our existence. This is the awareness that one's authentic, higher self is completely impervious to the ravages of any physical ailment whatever. The disease may regress or totally disappear when this awareness dawns, for reasons we may not understand. When this happens it comes as a gift, a blessing, and a grace—but again of secondary importance. The real cure is the realization that at the most essential level, we are all "untouchables"—utterly beyond the ravages of disease and death."[5]

Through his many books and tapes, Dr. Bernie Siegel has taken thousands of very ill people on a unique healing journey into the spiritual center of the mind. He has taught people exercises that can put them in touch with their inner self to effectuate healing of the body and soul. Dr. Siegel has observed that unhappiness, denial, and false attachment can be great impediments to wellness. He states, "Our emotions don't *happen* to us as much as we *choose* them. In fact, our own thoughts, emotions, and actions are the only things we really do control. In the first century A.D., the Greek thinker Epictetus made this fact the foundation of his philosophy, by declaring that all unhappiness arises from attempts to control events and other people, over which one has no power. The same futile attempt, born of our fears and resentments, weakens the body and leads to disease."[6]

---

[5] Larry Dossey, M.D., *Healing Words: The Power of Prayer and the Practice of Medicine* (San Francisco: HarperSanFrancisco, 1993), pp. 35–36.
[6] Bernie Siegel, M.D., *Love, Medicine & Miracles: Lessons Learned About Self-Healing from a Surgeon's Experience with Exceptional Patients* (New York: Harper & Row, 1986), pp. 190–191.

Dr. Martin Rossman, another pioneer of mind-body healing, further explains that the common roots of imaging and visualization shared by our species have been recognized by all cultures and traditions. Since the 1950s, researchers and clinicians throughout the world have studied the effectiveness and the role that imagery and visualization have played in recovery from illness. The consensus of these studies, which involved stress research, biofeedback, and relaxation therapies, supports the premise that the mind-body connection truly exists.

Dr. Rossman's therapy has many similarities with Buddhist meditation practices that use imagery. He introduces readers to the Simonton Method, a simple visualization technique that produces excellent results for seriously ill people. "The technique consisted of relaxing and picturing their immune cells as numerous, aggressive, and powerful, destroying the cancer cells which were visualized as isolated, weak and confused."[7]

Dr. Rossman presents easy-to-use scenarios to help people build their skills in relaxation and concentration. The Simonton Method teaches people to find a safe and peaceful inner place within their minds, then they learn to open up to the appearance of an inner advisor. They are encouraged to establish an ongoing dialogue with that inner advisor and to listen and carefully observe symbols from their meditation. This process enables people to gain an understanding of the true nature of their physical symptoms via their own images and symbols. The patients are then urged to use that imagery to induce self-healing. The Simonton Method has achieved significant results for all types of illness.

---

7 Martin Rossman, *Healing Yourself: A Step-by-Step Program for Better Health through Imagery* (New York: Walker & Co., 1987), p. 127.

Jon Kabat-Zinn, Ph.D., Director of The Stress Reduction Clinic at the University of Massachusetts has obtained excellent results using a technique known as "mindfulness meditation."

> Like other mind/body therapies, mindfulness meditation can induce deep states of relaxation, at times directly improve physical symptoms, and help patients lead full and satisfying lives. But while more familiar forms of meditation involve focusing on a sound, phrase, or prayer to minimize distracting thoughts, mindfulness does the opposite. In mindfulness meditation, you don't ignore distracting thoughts, sensations, or physical discomfort; instead, you focus on them. This form of practice is roughly 2,500 years old, stems primarily from the Buddhist tradition and was developed as a means of cultivating greater awareness and wisdom, with the aim of helping people live each moment of their lives—even the painful ones—as fully as possible. In our clinic, we have found that mindfulness practice can be beneficial for people facing a broad range of serious physical illness.[8]

Mindfulness meditation, like all Buddhist practices, has some degree of power, even when used outside the realm of faith and in a non-ecumenical manner for self-improvement. As an adjunct to conventional medical treatment, such meditation and yoga techniques may induce psychosomatic healing. However, they do not address the eradication of karmic illness originating in the

---

[8] Daniel Goleman and Joel Gurin, eds., *Mind Body Medicine: How to Use Your Mind for Better Health* (Yonkers, NY: Consumer Reports Books, 1993), pp. 260-261.

alaya consciousness or karmic storehouse because their healing powers do not originate from the amala consciousness of *Nam-myoho-renge-kyo*. Nichiren Daishonin states in his Gosho, "On Prolonging One's Life Span," that prayer based on the *Lotus Sutra* can conquer any illness:

> There are two types of illness: minor and serious. Early treatment by a skilled physician can cure even serious illness, not to mention minor ones. Karma also may be divided into two categories: fixed and unfixed. Sincere repentance will eradicate even immutable karma, to say nothing of karma that is unfixed

The power of faith and prayer to boost the immune system is indisputable, as demonstrated by Dr. Herbert Benson in his now-famous studies that proved the reality of "the relaxation response," the "faith factor," and "remembered wellness." All kinds of prayer, uttered faithfully, twice daily, produced measurable recuperative benefits. But what lies beyond the relaxation response, the faith factor, and remembered wellness is the province of *Nam-myoho-renge-kyo* and its power to positively transform karma, the inorganic origin of illness.

Right livelihood, responsible action, and devotion can help us maintain positive personal karma in this lifetime. What is paramount in Buddhist healing, however, is attending the effects of negative karma by drawing on the amala-vijnana—the source of all spiritual functions and the abode of the true entity of by chanting the Mystic Law, *Nam-myoho-renge-kyo* with all your heart.

---

9 Nichiren Daishonin, *The Writings of Nichiren Daishonin* (Tokyo: Soka Gakkai, 1999), p. 954.

CHAPTER 3

Mantra-Powered Visualization

The visualization technique is a combination of meditation and imagination. We should remember children's incredible "make-pretend" abilities. A child can pick up a twig and make it into a toy soldier or create a fort out of sand. There is much to learn from a child's imagination.

In general, mantra-powered visualization encourages us to imagine our bodies producing healing forces from within or, in some cases, attracting healing forces from outside of us, and, through the process of mind-over-matter, expedite the healing process. The idea is to visualize the area(s) in the body where there are problems. If there is a tumor in the bladder, you should learn where the bladder is located and what its basic functions are. If you have an entire system breakdown as with AIDS, lupus, or leukemia, concentrating on every cell in the body, one section at a time, is the suggested therapy.

When used to its highest degree, visualization is very much like the modern technology of virtual reality. With the inner eye and imagination, the body becomes a miniature universe where the voyager consciously travels throughout that domain, combating disease and restoring order through images and mental commands. Guided imagery used by therapists and medical professionals harnesses the power of suggestion and imagination to directly confront disease. The mind has the power to heal the body through the power of suggestion—of that there is little doubt.

Lotus Sutra based, mantra-powered visualization brings into focus the conventional therapeutic practices of visualization used by healthcare professionals, but it also provides its users with a mystic power that originates beyond the senses in the ultimate depths of being. Mantra-powered visualization is a precise, deliberate exercise that will produce extraordinary results in both body and mind. Moreover, it is a doorway to a spiritual path of enormous benefit. Putting our preconceptions aside, all we need do is break loose from the dogmatic fetters that impede new knowledge and spiritual growth.

For me, mantra-powered visualization was a powerful tool against illness, when I wasn't even strong enough to pick up a hammer. Words have power. Some might scoff at the ability of some strange sounding words to produce such exciting results. Just the phrases "I love you," or "I hate you," have a powerful effect on our psyche. It is imperative that we strengthen our ability to take firm control of our mind through the determination of our spirit, especially when our body seems to be doing the opposite of what we consciously want it to. At the core of our being is a master physician, a "medicine king," if you will, who can quicken recovery with the help of your doctor.

The use of mantra-powered visualization advances meditation from a placid void into a dynamically active meditative force. Focusing the mind on chanting minimizes outside distractions, and helps us attain and maintain concentration. Many Buddhists in America first learned of mantra-powered visualization through reading a lecture series called "The Key to Revitalization" in the Buddhist journal, *Seikyo Times* by Soka Gakkai International Vice-President, Takehisa Tsuji.[1] Mr. Tsuji is far too humble to take credit for melding the modern medical therapy of visualization with the essence of the *Lotus Sutra*, but the fact is that his guidance on fighting illness with daimoku (chanting *Nam-myoho-renge-kyo*) and visualization has helped thousands of people all over the world. In one of his lectures, he quoted from Nichiren Daishonin's orally transmitted teachings, "Ongi Kuden," to make his point that daimoku is our body and life itself: "Our head is *myo*, our neck is *ho*, our breast is *ren*, our stomach is *ge*, and our legs are *kyo*. This five-foot body of ours is the five characters of *Myoho-renge-kyo*."[2]

THE MANTRA PRONUNCIATION
AND VISUALIZATION

Each syllable of *Nam-myoho-renge-kyo* corresponds to a specific area of the human form in relationship to the life energy conduits

1 See Takehisa Tsuji, "Buddhism and Medicine," issue no. 206, pp. 48–50 and "The Key to Revitalization," installment 1, pp. 37–39 and installment 11, issue no. 243, pp. 40–42, in the *Seikyo Times*.
2 Nichiren Daishonin, "Explanation of the Hoben-bon, Part 3," in *Gosho Zenshu* (Tokyo: Soka Gakkai, 1952), p. 716.

or spiritual energy centers known in Vedic cosmology and Tantric Buddhism as the *chakras*. *Nam* can be envisioned as originating above the head at the seventh level of the *sahasrara chakra*, like a crown of light that emanates toward the heavens and cascades down, surrounding the body like a golden robe of holy light. *Myo* is located between the eyes at the level of the *ajna chakra*. *Ho* is in the throat, corresponding to the *visuddha chakra*. *Ren* is the *anahata chakra* in the center of the chest, and *Ge* is the *manipura chakra* at the point of the navel. *Kyo* embodies both the *svadhisthana chakra* at the level of the genitals and *muladhara chakra* at the base of the spine.

Nam-myoho-renge-kyo is pronounced:

Nam	as in Tom
Myo	as in me-oh
Ho	as in go
Ren	as in the bird, "wren"
Ge	as in gay
Kyo	as in key-oh

Each syllable of daimoku corresponds to a specific area of the human form:

Myo	head
Ho	throat
Ren	chest
Ge	abdomen
Kyo	extremities (arms, legs, hands, and feet)

Nam does not correspond to a specific part of the anatomy but surrounds the body and spirit, connecting it with the universe. You repeat the words *Nam-myo-ho-ren-ge-kyo* out loud, slowly at first. While chanting, you formulate a mental picture of an attack upon the disease.

The easiest method of mantra-powered visualization to begin with is concentrating only on the words and the corresponding place in the body. Start by thinking: *Myo* (head), *Ho* (throat), *Ren* (chest), *Ge* (abdomen), *Kyo* (extremities). When repeating the words, create a mental picture of placing each word's sound at the corresponding area of your body. Where you have medical problems in your body, increase your emphasis and concentration on the corresponding word and place.

For example, if you have a polyp in the colon, when you get to that area you would exert increased mental and spiritual energies in pronouncing the word *Ge*. It's like adding torque when trying to finish tightening a nut and bolt. Every time you get back to the word and area of *Ge*, you add emphasis to that pronunciation.

HOW TO CHANT

Before we advance into specific techniques, it is important to understand that prayer is not a technique—it is the natural action of desire. We pray because we desire to get well or express our appreciation to the absolute. We pray for certain things to happen in our life. Prayer is a simple act that is available to everyone. Exactly how we pray is in many cases very different.

If you are ambulatory and can sit up, do your chanting while seated in a comfortable chair. If you are bedridden, lying in whatever position is most comfortable for you will suffice. Place your hands before your chest (or on your chest if you are lying down), with all your fingers touching in the prayer position (or, if lying down, place one hand over the other on your chest). Begin repeating *Nam-myoho-renge-kyo* over and over and out loud (if possible).

To begin mantra-powered visualization, concentrate on getting the pronunciation and rhythm of the words right. Begin chanting with identical emphasis on each word, as if you were a steam engine train starting out: chug (*Nam*)...chug (*Myo*)...chug (*Ho*)...chug (*Ren*)...chug (*Ge*)...chug (*Kyo*). Your speed will naturally increase, just like a train gathering momentum. With experience, you will decide upon the pace that is most comfortable for you. I recommend that your chanting should eventually have the same rhythm and speed as a galloping horse.

You might feel you can't say the words out loud because you fear you might disturb others, or you might be too weak or incapable of speaking. If you are in a situation where you can repeat the words out loud, you should. However, it's okay if you can only whisper the words. If you are not able to say the words aloud or whisper them, you can still obtain complete benefit by using your inner voice to loudly proclaim the words.

At first, repeating words that sound strange or foreign may seem awkward. In the beginning, you might have to exert considerable effort to visualize a scenario, repeat the words correctly, and maintain that vision for any sustained length of time. Whenever possible, try to perform mantra-powered visualization for at least ten minutes at a time. After you build up endurance and stamina, you will benefit most from sessions of twenty minutes or longer, performed twice daily. The ideal times to chant are in the morning and in the evening. However, any time of the day, when distractions are minimal, is fine.

MANTRA-POWERED VISUALIZATION EXERCISE

The following breaks up the techniques of mantra-powered visualization into easy-to-learn exercise segments. Experienced chanters will spend only a second on each syllable of the mantra. If you are weak or have chronic breathing problems, you will probably have difficulty doing that. It's okay—just hold each syllable for as long as you can.

1. Either sit upright or lie down to begin the exercise, depending on your physical condition, and what's most comfortable for you. Whenever possible, sit upright without slouching, placing your hands in front of your chest and joining your fingers together in a prayer position. If you must lie down, place your hands, one over the other, on your chest in a mummy-like position, then relax.

2. Close your eyes and quietly visualize the inside of your body. Thank your body and its components. The purpose of this process is to help you become more in tune with your own body and facilitate the concept that the body and mind work together with your spiritual nature to restore health. By cultivating this dialogue between the mind and body, both come into harmony.

3. Say the first part of the mantra, *Nam*. *Nam* is the beginning word and the vibration that motivates incredibly powerful forces. Chant the word *Nam,* imagining your body surrounded by golden light.

4. Moving from *Nam,* strongly chant the word *Myo,* holding that sound for about one beat. The light you imagined in

41

Nam now moves to *Myo*, which corresponds to the head. Everything associated with the head is included in the word *Myo*. The sound, vibration, and light of *Myo* resound inside and about your head.

5. After holding and intoning the word *Myo* for one beat, you move to *Ho*, holding that for one beat. *Ho* governs the throat. Imagine the sound vibrating there. As your visualization skills improve, you might imagine light radiating inside your throat, ready to stream down throughout the rest of your body.

6. After saying *Ho*, take a new breath and say *Ren*. Allowing the sound of *Ren* to expand in the area of the chest, hold that sound for a beat, imagining the sound and light growing in strength. Inhale.

7. Exhaling, say the word *Ge*. *Ge* is the stomach area and everything inside it. Hold that sound for a beat, imagining the light that has been moving down from your head and chest is now resting in your stomach, glowing radiantly. Inhale.

8. After exhaling again, inhale and say the word *Kyo* with strength and vitality. *Kyo* is the legs, feet, arms, and hands. Allow the light to move through your body. Once again, go to the top and say the word *Nam* and begin the process over.

USING VISUALIZATION

The mastery of visualization combined with chanting is not a prerequisite of healing yourself. At first it may be far too difficult to remember how to create a healing image and how the words correspond to the body. Chanting is the first priority, creating the image is secondary. Chanting *is* prayer. What your hopes and fears are will emerge.

As I teach people who have difficulty with adding visualization to their prayer, I have witnessed that they automatically create their own unique approaches. For example, a person who begins to chant and can just manage to remember the words and pronounce them correctly might begin by seeing his or her diabetic ulcer or tumor in his or her mind's eye. An image of that problem area will appear and the person might then spontaneously imagine that the words and thoughts have automatically centered on those areas with a corresponding image. In effect, they have jumped right to the essence of how to perform the therapy.

For many people, visualizing heavenly light, imagining vivid disease-fighting scenarios, or concentrating on anything complex will be very difficult. At first, it may be impossible to do much of anything beyond mastering the pronunciation of the words. As with anything new, it is important to learn the basics and move at your own speed toward developing greater skills.

Producing results with mantra-powered visualization is not predicated on the complexity or the greatness of your imagery. The benefits derived from this form of visualization are based on effort, sincerity, and an inquisitive mind. This is not like an exercise regimen that builds body muscles based on resistance and repetition. Because daimoku is spiritual in origin and mystic by nature, the results emerge from a different sphere.

Although there are countless visualization scenarios that you can create, choose a scenario that has some kind of emotional impact for you. Once you "build" the visualization, let go of the image and your illness, and let healing happen. The following are visualization scenarios that people have used successfully.

Nam-myo-ho-ren-ge-kyo **is like the raging sea.** The pounding waves crashing into the shore are the force that wears away a tumor or washes out body poisons. The undertow of the powerful waves pulls out toxins or suctions out cancer cells.

Nam-myo-ho-ren-ge-kyo **is shot out of a great laser canon at tumors or abnormalities.** If you have bone deterioration or broken bones, you can have your lasers shoot rays of *Nam-myo-ho-ren-ge-kyo* that are restorative, bonding, or able to stimulate growth. You can decide what kind of rays to shoot.

Nam-myo-ho-ren-ge-kyo **can be the warm and moist wash cloth your mother used to bathe you when you were a child.** The cloth can contain mystical healing powers. You can go to any part in your body and soothe the pain and heal the wound.

Nam-myo-ho-ren-ge-kyo **can be a vacuum cleaner;** a broom, a spray device, or anything that can help you visualize the removing of disease, bringing gentle or acute healing to the areas of concern.

Nam-myo-ho-ren-ge-kyo **can be electric charges,** beams of light, torpedoes, six-shooter guns, arrows, even your own hands strangling the daylights out of a cancerous tumor.

Nam-myoho-renge-kyo can cure and reverse any illness without the added methodology of visualization. Chanting based on faith is completely adequate to bring forth all the magnificent benefits of Buddhism. However, many people, even Buddhists experienced in meditation, need to use visualization as a separate and supplemental practice in order to expunge diseases from the body and mind. Here, I am explaining mantra-powered visualization as both a prayer and a spiritual tool to eliminate disease.

I am reminded of an experience that I had around 1996, when a friend approached me for help. Mr. G. was a 45-year-old African-American who was a sheriff's deputy for our local drug task force. On a daily basis, he was called upon to put his life at risk. He was also expected to protect the lives of his fellow officers. His agility was essential for everyone's safety. He was a big man, over 270 pounds of solid muscle. In his college days, Mr. G. had played football as a starting offensive guard for the University of Illinois and had taken so many hits that, over time, he developed chronic bursitis in his left shoulder. For a week he was in agony. He had received injections of cortisone for years and his physician was now recommending surgery if the pain came back. Being a devout southern Baptist, he had gone to his reverend for healing, but the problem persisted.

Despite his religious beliefs and reservations, he asked me to help him. I told him to close his eyes, concentrate on my words, and imagine the source of his pain. I told him to imagine that the area where the pain originated was being bathed in healing light. I put my hand on his shoulder and began to chant *Nam-myoho-renge-kyo*, imagining its cosmic energy flowing through my hand into him. He also said daimoku in a quiet voice. Never had I been more entranced in the power of prayer. I had never tried to lay on hands before, but adapted my approach to an expedient means that he could readily relate to as a Baptist. I felt powerful currents of vital energy flowing out of my hand into him. After five minutes, I disengaged the healing and told him to come back the next day. When Mr. G. saw me the next day, his shoulder was back to normal with no pain whatsoever. I have seen him perhaps a dozen times over a five-year period, and he insists that the pain vanished that day and never returned.

I ascribe Mr. G.'s recovery to his desire to be healed, not to any supernatural ability of my own. He wanted to be healed and chanted with me; his personal faith in God and his religion never wavered.

PRAYING FOR OTHERS

One of the most important aspects of mantra-powered visualization is its power to affect a loved one, even if they are unable to use it for themselves. We can use mantra-powered visualization to direct healing powers at a loved one and in so doing improve the disposition of that person, while helping them to bring forth strength and benefit from within themselves.

You may wonder how using this meditative technique for another person can work? People frequently describe their chanting as being able to beneficially influence the life of another person, even thousands of miles away, without that person's knowledge. Repeating daimoku into someone's ear if they are in a coma or using visualization to guide the mind into the sphere of consciousness and induce healing can be learned with practice and an open mind.

HOW TO WORD YOUR PRAYERS

The prayers and good thoughts for someone suffering from illness are a potent force that can affect the condition of a person on the other end of the world without the slightest delay or impediment. Not only is prayer "nonlocal," it is an act of our will and an aspect of cosmic energy that interpenetrates all phenomena according to that will. Prayer can also be seen as an expression of quantum consciousness from the depths of life that has the power to heal, help, and even harm. The mystic organizing force of the universe that responds to our prayers is completely nonjudgmental and quite literal. For this reason, the scientific experts on prayer, such as the prayer research group Spindrift, herald the efficacy of nonspecific and open-ended prayers for a variety of reasons. The most obvious reason to use open-ended, nonspecific prayers is that we don't truly know what is best for our lives. Another reason is that since prayer is answered literally, if we phrase our prayer the wrong way, we may get exactly what we asked for, but in ways we did not expect or want. Dr. Larry Dossey encourages people to preface their prayer with "Thy will be done." Another more neutral prayer approach he suggests is "May the best result happen." It is truly difficult to know what is best for ourselves or someone else when viewed from the standpoint of the eternity of life.

As a practicing Buddhist in the Chicago area for nearly three decades, I have constantly been around people who pray a lot. I have listened to hundreds if not thousands of personal faith-based experiences of people praying for their desires and to overcome their problems. In all that time, I have never heard anyone proclaim that they had a problem or a goal in mind and prayed for the best result, leaving their fate up to Buddha, God or the universe. Invariably, everyone's experience that I heard or learned of secondhand had a specific target or desire in mind and prayed for a specific result. When they prayed in that way, the best result for their life naturally occurred.

If we accept the experts' methods of using nonspecific prayers, we relinquish control of our destiny to an external power that seems greater than ourselves. It is very difficult to pray for the best result when we have a strong determination for a specific outcome. For this reason, I firmly believe that nonspecific and open-ended prayer is in some respects unnatural, as it overrides the object of our desires for whatever God the universe deems us worthy to receive. I am quite sure that in the long run we get what we need. Since the universe is nonjudgmental and responds accordingly to prayer, it is best to give deep thought to how our prayers are structured and what is truly in our heart. Nichiren gives a fine example of praying for someone's health with a specific result in mind:

> When the steward of this district sent me a request for his recovery from illness, I wondered if I should accept it. But since he showed some degree of faith in me, I decided I would appeal to the *Lotus Sutra* . . . I was sure that they [protective forces] would consider my request and show some sign. Certainly they would never forsake me, but would respond as attentively as a person rubs a sore or scratches an itch. And as it turned out, the steward recovered.[3]

---

[3] Nichiren Daishonin, "The Izu Exile," in *The Writings of Nichiren Daishonin* (Tokyo: Soka Gakkai, 1999), pp. 35–36.

In 1264, Nichiren learned that his mother was critically ill. He later wrote about praying for her recovery after he had returned home from visiting her: "When I prayed for my mother, not only was her illness cured, but her life was prolonged by four years."[4]

MANTRA-POWERED VISUALIZATION FOR PAIN MANAGEMENT

The pain of disease and injury is a serious problem for both patients and clinicians. Although pain protects us by alerting us about a problem, no one wants prolonged physical pain. Mantra-powered visualization can be an important tool in pain management because it helps us induce the brain to produce more of its own pain-fighting chemicals, such as endorphins.

To use mantra-powered visualization to relieve pain, you direct your attention to the localized areas and "send" *Nam-myoho-renge-kyo* there with powerful bursts of energy. When generalized pain is present, you could imagine torrents of fresh spring water cascading down your body, from head to toe, providing cooling relief. In the case of traumatic pain from a serious injury, the mind is often overwhelmed and can think of nothing else. However, you can block out pain just as if a shot of morphine had been administered. By *not* ignoring pain, but focusing on it with the mantra, you can eventually bring that pain under control to a tolerable level.

You can accomplish pain management by using the same technique of directing the mantra toward the corresponding

4 Nichiren Daishonin, "On Prolonging One's Life Span," in *The Writings of Nichiren Daishonin*, p. 955.

areas of the body. When you have a headache, which is in the area of *myo,* you would emphasize *myo*; and if your feet hurt, you would add energy to *kyo.* By visualizing the area of pain or discomfort and directing healing energies there, even intractable pain can be neutralized.

The following ten points are a summary of mantra-powered visualization:

1. Make the determination to win against disease by using mantra-powered visualization based on faith.

2. Learn the pronunciation of the words and commit them to memory.

3. Find the right place and right time to begin your exercise.

4. Thank your body, its systems, and organs.

5. Repeat *Nam-myoho-renge-kyo* while concentrating on your body one section at a time.

6. Allow the sound of the words to vibrate in the corresponding body areas.

7. Eliminate distractions by continually chanting *Nam-myoho-renge-kyo.*

8. Visualize a preselected scenario and attack your disease by using your imagination and meditation.

9. Use mantra-powered visualization ten minutes at a time, twice daily, increasing the time of usage according to your ability.

10. At night, when you go to bed, while you are between wake-

fulness and sleep, quietly commune with your body, going through the different sections one at a time, like a CT (computer tomography) scanner might do. Congratulate your body for its marvelous work.

Because the Mystic Law works on a seemingly incomprehensible level, chanting frequently produces conspicuous results for the benefit of those people closest to the person who harnesses it. In other words, a person who is very ill and faithfully takes up mantra-powered visualization to the best of their ability may die in their brave battle, but the heroic nature of their struggle and their disposition at the moment of death will produce greater results in those surrounding them than a thousand scholarly books of eloquent theory. With their own eyes, loved ones will witness the profound effect that the Mystic Law has on someone fighting for their life.

Mantra-powered visualization is a technique that directs the focus and control to the latent powers within. Because that force originates within all people, it can be used by anyone regardless of their beliefs.

At the moment a person intones daimoku, their negative karma is sent through a veritable rock crusher, and their dominant life condition is challenged. If their typical life condition was Anger, the cause of the Tenth World of Buddhahood (enlightenment) is seemingly placed on top of that Anger, driving it into latency. When the person stops chanting the mantra, their dominant life condition reacts with the environment and tries to emerge once again. Each time a person uses the Mystic Law, the foundation of the dominant world of Anger is transformed into its enlightened aspect, eventually giving way to the elevated conditions of Learning, Realization, Altruism, and Enlightenment.

The emergence of the higher life conditions of learning, realization, altruism, and enlightenment has a marked influence on the person's outlook and ability to gain perspective on their illness and inner life. Physical, mental and spiritual benefits frequently begin to appear in the improvement of health and attitude. As the person begins to change inside, their optimism in overcoming illness grows.

CHAPTER 4

Experiences of Challenging Illness

Chanting frequently and with great passion is the key to absolute victory, especially when confronting chronic illness. The following are some experiences from people who used *Nam-myoho-renge-kyo* and visualization to overcome illness.

PAIN OF FIBROMYALGIA

At 44 years of age, Ms. J. was diagnosed, after six months of medical evaluation, with fibromyalgia syndrome. Fibromyalgia is an all-pervading ache in the muscles, accompanied by local pain that occurs when pressure is applied to specific body areas. Some of the conditions she routinely suffered from were chronic rhinitis, easy bruising, night cramps, restless leg syndrome, sleep apnea, dry eyes and mouth, bruxism, photophobia, PMS, many infections, hair loss, generalized muscular stiffness, "foggy" brain, dyslexia, panic attacks, mood swings, irritability, a feeling of her hands and feet being swollen without evidence of fluid retention, and widespread muscular pain.

Having been told that there was no cure, she decided the best approach was to first manage the pain, then work on the other symptoms. Ms. J. used an approach to visualization that encompassed her whole body. She first got herself into a relaxed position, either sitting or reclining. She then visualized her whole body and, slowly reciting the mantra, concentrated on individual parts. Her technique was as follows:

1. While saying *Nam* she visualized her whole body encompassed in a soft, white, cloud-like light.

2. As she said *Myo* she visualized the area of her head becoming brighter, and then with *Ho,* her throat area became bright.

3. Because she suffered from severe pain in the neck, chest, and back, she visualized *Ren* as a brighter, warmer light in those areas.

4. Moving on to *Ge* for the hip region, she felt the light continue to become brighter and warmer.

5. Her arms, hands, legs, and feet experienced the most pain to the extent that she could not walk across the room sometimes without holding on to furniture, or had no feeling in her hands or feet. While concentrating on *Kyo,* she saw the bright, warm light travel throughout her extremities and pulse like gentle hands massaging her painful limbs.

After rhythmically repeating this mantra-powered visualization, she could actually feel her skin become warm and her muscles relax. She practiced this technique over a period of several months, at which point she became so attuned to her body that sometimes, literally within minutes, her pain would disappear. After about six months of practicing this form of pain management, she was virtually free of the fibromyalgia symptoms.

BATTLING CANCER

Mrs. T., a 50-year-old woman, had been a Buddhist for more than twenty years. She was the mother of two teenagers and had lived in Connecticut for many years. Mrs. T. was under a considerable amount of duress between 1993 and 1994. She was slowly recovering from a severe head trauma, her husband was suffering from two polyps in his colon, and her older brother, Mr. P., was experiencing a recurrence of a rare and often deadly lymphoma in his upper spine. I taught her how to use mantra-powered visualization so she could teach it to her brother, who was about to begin his first round of a new experimental chemotherapy called ICE (ifosfamide, carboplatin, and etoposide).

Mr. P., who lived in New Jersey, was not a religious person but was open to spirituality. Expressing a willingness to try anything to get rid of his cancer, he allowed his sister and brother-in-law to teach him how to use the techniques they had learned. Together, and according to their respective capacities, each one began using mantra-powered visualization. Each person subsequently experienced some degree of benefit relative to their condition. Mrs. T. was able to quicken the healing process of the soft tissue in her neck, as well as of her skull and nerves. Making remarkable progress, she began assisting other severely injured and impaired patients in her neurological clinic, teaching them to use mantra-powered visualization—with the full cooperation of her doctor and therapist.

Mr. P. used mantra-powered visualization to fight his cancer, although he was inexperienced in chanting. Thanks to excellent medical treatment and mantra-powered visualization, his lymphoma went into remission. Although his cancer returned, Mr. P. had put his affairs in order and faced the end with dignity and courage. With his sister by his side, they both chanted to his final moment. Mr. P. died without pain or distress, completely in control of his mind, and in a state of tranquillity.

Mr. W., a 68-year-old African-American who lived in central Illinois, provided another example of how using mantra-powered visualization can help us to deal with cancer. He had been diagnosed with metastatic prostate cancer that had invaded his bones. He was declared terminal by his doctor, sent home with pain pills and vitamins. After reading an article about Buddhist healing, as a last resort, his son brought Mr. W. to my office. At that meeting Mr. W. was jaundiced, emaciated, depressed, and in extreme pain. He impressed me as a brave man who knew he was going to die. But he was determined to spend quality time with all of his five children who were returning home from all over the country to visit him, one at a time.

I taught Mr. W. and his son how to chant and use visualization, and counseled them on the eternity of life and how life could possibly be prolonged, so he might be able to die with dignity, at a time of his own choosing. Mr. W., who had been a devout Christian all his life, saw no conflict with his religious beliefs in chanting *Nam-myoho-renge-kyo* to fight the pain of cancer, and end his life with dignity, on his own terms. He confessed that he was depressed because he thought his time would run out before he could see all his children. Two months later, Mr. W. called to set an appointment to see me because he had something important to discuss.

He explained that he had just returned from a scheduled doctor's appointment and his PSA (prostate specific antigen) test indicated that he was disease free. His doctor was both elated and at a loss for an explanation of Mr. W.'s remission and rebound. Mr. W. had gained weight, looked joyful, and he had completely lost his jaundiced appearance. Mr. W. expressed heartfelt gratitude for his remission and attributed it to his chanting of *Nam-myoho-renge-kyo.*

I was amazed. He then told me that a week after our visit he was stricken with pain in his bones and stomach that was so severe, he couldn't even cry out to his son who was in the next room—he was literally paralyzed with pain. Mr. W. somehow composed himself and remembered to chant *Nam-myoho-renge-kyo* while visualizing the pain flowing out of his mouth like thousands of bats flying from a cave, expelling the pain with each labored breath. Mr. W. thought he chanted only five minutes, but it seemed like hours. After those five minutes the pain simply vanished. The next evening the pain did not return and he began to feel more energetic with each passing day. Excitement and appreciation due to the possibility that he might actually live to see all his children flooded his senses. Over the next month, he remained symptom free and most importantly, he was pain free.

Mr. W. was able to say goodbye to all his children. Mr. W. said that because of chanting he had accomplished what he set out to do. Five days later, after all his children had gone home, he suddenly felt ill and checked into the hospital. On his first night in the hospital he fell asleep and passed away. His death was pain free and peaceful, as if he had taken a well-deserved nap after working in his garden.

BREAST CANCER

Ms. G. was a 51-year-old woman from Chicago who was diagnosed with cancer in her right breast. The doctors believed that it had spread, but could find no evidence in their x-rays or lymph node biopsy. She had a lumpectomy. Prior to the beginning of radiation treatments, she sought out my advice and I taught her mantra-powered visualization. She had chanted for twelve years and knew that other people had overcome all kinds of health problems, including cancer, with their faith and prayer. Although fearful of the unknown, she had a strong determination to show positive proof of the power of faith and chanting.

Ms. G.'s visualization while chanting consisted of seeing *Nam-myoho-renge-kyo* as intelligent laser beams that zapped errant cells, much like the "Star Wars" defense system might target and destroy an enemy missile. She knew that the place of her primary tumor was in her chest, but no one knew if any cancerous cells had migrated to other parts of her body. Throughout her entire radiation treatment, she refined her visualization, attempting to search for the disease and urge her immune system to eliminate every last cancer cell.

When her treatments were finished, and her follow-up appointments showed no further signs of cancer, she cut back on her mantra-powered visualization practice. About a year later, she had a mammogram that revealed a small mass in her left breast. She was scheduled for a biopsy. Several days before the actual biopsy, Ms. G., again sought my advice on how to use mantra-powered visualization to rid her life of cancer, once and for all. She decided to construct a new visualization that would go to the molecular level of her disease.

Ms. G. knew that all spiritual functions emerged from the amala consciousness, the innermost core of life, and that the alaya consciousness was the storehouse of karma. After reviewing the actions of her life, she realized that the cancer must have had its karmic origins in a previous life, but she would never know for sure exactly what actions had created such karma. She apologized to the universe for whatever it was that she had done. Beginning her prayer in that way, she enacted a new visualization scenario based on the quantum world's peculiar nature of particles existing one moment and not existing the next. This time, she viewed the area where the mass was located and saw the mass as molecules that were out of vibration with the rest of her body. Her mind then became a beacon of *Nam-myoho-renge-kyo* that emitted a calibrating pulse that would bring those molecules comprising the mass into resonance with the healthy cells in her body. She envisioned the process like a tuning fork being used to tune a violin. She dedicated twenty minutes twice daily to her visualization until it was time for her biopsy.

Her oncologist had new x-rays taken the morning of the biopsy. Ms. G was shocked when her doctor told her that he was canceling the biopsy because the suspicious image that had appeared on the x-ray did not show up in the computer analysis. The mass was now so small that it was virtually undetectable. Ms. G. was told to come back in six months. Although she was not given a clean bill of health, she was overjoyed. The fact that her original cancer had not returned and the newly discovered mass seemed to have rapidly shrunk into a shadow, undetectable by the latest computer technology, was proof to her that mantra-powered visualization was a powerful adjunct to her overall care.

DIABETIC ULCERS

Mr. R. was a 40-year-old Hispanic American whose debilitating diabetes forced him to relocate from Los Angeles to central Illinois to live with his father. Mr. R. had developed recurring ulcers on his feet that required constant care, rendering him hardly able to walk and, therefore, unable to do physical labor. He followed a strict diet, took insulin injections, continually monitored his feet, and seemed to be constantly taking medicine to fight off infection. But the ulcers would not go away. In a last-ditch effort to overcome his foot ulcers, Mr. R. asked me to teach him how to use mantra-powered visualization. He imagined his feet being bathed in healing light that was cool and refreshing. He made a determination that the ulcers would be gone in seven days, when he was required to return to his doctor. Afraid of developing gangrene and losing his feet, he made a powerful effort to produce healing images in his mind while he chanted.

Each day, he would look under the bandages to inspect the ulcers and each day he would see a small improvement. The morning of his trip to the doctor he was surprised to see that during the night the ulcers had completely healed. His foot ulcers never returned.

COMA

Miss M. was an 11-year-old Hispanic living in the U.S. While on vacation with family in Mexico, she was involved in a serious car accident. She was thrown through the windshield and landed on the pavement, suffering a severe head trauma and broken pelvis. At the scene of the accident, she went into convulsions. On her way to the hospital, she had a second convulsion. Although Miss M.'s mother and stepfather were in the United States, they rushed to her bedside within 24 hours. Miss M. was in a coma. Her parents were Buddhists and so they began to chant *Nam-myoho-renge-kyo* in her ears the moment they arrived. The child was familiar with the words but she didn't move or respond to anything for two weeks.

Her doctors were worried about blood in her skull near her brain, fearing it could evolve into a potentially fatal clot. Buddhists from the United States chanted for her survival and recovery. Before she was transferred to a hospital in the U.S., CT scans indicated that the blood near her brain had disappeared. After a month in intensive care, she was released as an outpatient. Her mental capacities are now excellent, she has not had any of the seizures that are common to that type of trauma, and her body has healed itself quickly.

Miss M., her mother, and father are all convinced that *Nam-myoho-renge-kyo* was responsible for her quick recovery. The doctors could only wait and see because neither surgery nor medicine could solve her problem. She remembers nothing of the accident or her first month of hospitalization, but she vividly remembers the sweet sound of chanting in her ear.

HIGH BLOOD PRESSURE

At 38 years of age, Ms. L. was diagnosed with hypertension. She worked as an office manager and had been a Buddhist for more than a decade. Her mother had a long history of high blood pressure and her father suffered from heart disease. Although she was on medication, Ms. L.'s blood pressure ranged around 145 over 95. Concerned that she would someday be a stroke victim, or suffer from other kinds of cardiovascular disease, she used mantra-powered visualization in an attempt to lower her blood pressure. Because of financial problems, Ms. L. could no longer afford her medication so she began chanting while monitoring her blood pressure at home. Within several weeks her blood pressure readings dropped to within the normal range of 120 over 80 and has remained there since 1994, with no medication. When she returned to her doctor and explained her situation, he was quite concerned that she stopped taking the medication without his approval. But he was very pleased that her blood pressure had returned to safe levels. Today she continues to use mantra-powered visualization and requires no medication to control her blood pressure.

EMOTIONAL DIFFICULTIES

Ms. K., a 43-year-old Native American, was going through a very emotional and difficult time. She wanted to replace the neg-

ative emotions she was feeling with positive emotions. She used
the following technique:

1. She put herself into a relaxed state, either sitting or reclining.

2. She visualized her whole body as having a "negative" color
   (in her case, orange).

3. She visualized the unwanted emotions swirling around in the
   orange color and attached names to them such as negativity,
   fear, rage, low self-esteem, low confidence, grief, vindictiveness, revenge, and sadness.

4. As she began to recite the mantra, she visualized each of the
   negative emotions being pushed out by a "positive" color (in
   her case, blue) and watched as her body slowly changed from
   the negative color to the positive color.

5. As the positive color filled up her body, she visualized new,
   positive emotions taking over the negative, and attached
   names to them such as optimism, courage, confidence,
   absolute happiness, and strength.

She repeated this visualization once or twice a day until her life
condition became lighter and she was able to replace the negativity with positive and forward-looking emotions.

THE PRAYER MATRIX

Maintaining a balance between the best medical treatment and
the power of faith and prayer is only common sense. It is the
physician's role to treat and cure illness wherever possible, and it

is our responsibility to live a healthy lifestyle, mustering up the determination to change our health problems for the better, especially when an illness eludes a physician's ability to cure.

Prayer is a mystery. It gives us strength when we are troubled and enables us to influence matters seemingly out of our control. Prayer is a tool, a shield, a weapon, and a heartfelt expression of our inseparable connection to the ultimate spiritual reality of the universe. Prayer is appreciation, determination, apology, devotion, and our private confessional. My spiritual mentor, Daisaku Ikeda, suggests that prayer preceded formal religion. From that perspective, prayer is one of the most basic, natural functions of human beings.

I do not discount the sincerity, validity, or effectiveness of anyone's prayers, religion, or spiritual beliefs. I have merely presented the *Lotus Sutra*'s essence as a unique possibility for people engaged in their own efforts to challenge illness and suffering. I do not claim that any one method of prayer, technique, or healing philosophy is better than another. My belief is that actual proof is superior to documentary or theoretical proof. Since this form of healing is virtually unknown and unstudied, the only evidence of its greatness are the words of the Buddha himself, and the many anecdotal experiences of Nichiren Buddhists in the Soka Gakkai International. For that reason, I have detailed my personal experience in overcoming advanced cancer in Part II of this book so it can be added to the record.

I have explained in detail how to use chanting and visualization to challenge illness and suffering. Prayer is a vast concept. Prayer encompasses chanting, all types of meditation, spoken prayer in conversational form with God(s) or the absolute—even our random thoughts and desires are a form of prayer. Our consciousness is an expression of cosmic life and prayer is the means for us to fuse with that energy.

Even though you may have different beliefs and circumstances, I have presented you the Buddha's prescribed means of communication with the absolute. It is my hope that you will use modern Buddhist healing to challenge and overcome all suffering, illness, and fear of death. *Nam-myoho-renge-kyo.*

PART TWO

MY
BATTLE

CHAPTER 5

Double Tiger

ancer is a "double tiger." One tiger attacks our relationship with the world, while inside, we face a merciless beast of fear and pain. How can a person kill a wild tiger like cancer? What strategy can be used against such brute force?

Like a fierce tiger, cancer must be respected. My story is one of a warrior who tried to slip past a mighty foe, but was forced to fight instead. In the fight against a mortal enemy like cancer, there is only one survivor. The nature of the battle is inherently unfair. Even with excellent medicine, the challenge to win is formidable.

I am an American Buddhist, but I am telling my story for my non-Buddhist brothers and sisters who seek a different spiritual point of view to help them regain their health. My fight against cancer was waged with the weapons of the mind, the voice, the inner eye, and the imagination of a child. While my doctors used poison agents to cure my illness, I used grand optimism, communion with my body, faith, and mantra-powered visualization.

Actual proof is superior to argument. The fact that I survived advanced Hodgkin's disease cannot be denied. How I overcame this disease is of vital importance for anyone suffering from cancer, AIDS, mental disorder, and all maladies. The burning question of my quest for survival was: "How could a person of modest ability and station bring the message of healing to the people of the world?" I have no recognized credentials beyond thirty years as a professional writer, and being a cancer survivor. Through the grueling journey of survival, it all became quite obvious.

The joy or pain of the present instantly becomes the past, and the past is no more than a dream, no matter what our experience of it was. The future is not fixed; we create it with our will and pure imagination. We must not let the past control the present. For the cancer patient and others suffering from chronic illness it is important to seize the moment with freedom and volition. By doing so, we may learn how to save our own life.

As with any long journey, I ask you to travel light. My intention is to tell a story of fighting cancer with the amazing Mystic Law of *Nam-myoho-renge-kyo*. Let the skeptics have their laugh at us, and let others proceed as they will in their fight for recovery. Don't let the strange-sounding words or Eastern ideas deter you from the place of reward, for the ideas are universal in application. Our mission is to gain empowerment and regain control of our life. In all great undertakings, huge obstacles will appear, one after another, trying to stop our forward progress. My story is a blueprint for perseverance and victory. Those who listen will benefit greatly.

INSTANT KARMA

Lurking around every corner are the brutal realities of life. After an immense struggle to enhance the quality of life for my family and having obtained a modicum of career success, I was blind-sided by one of the most dangerous and powerful enemies known to humankind. Cancer struck me like lightning from a cloudless sky. Without warning, I went from a rugged physical specimen to an emaciated, feeble old man in the space of a few months. What looked like a plummet into unhappiness and death turned into the most important event of my life, and put me in touch with people all over the world.

Having a limited understanding of what advanced cancer implied, I faced a difficult and uncertain future. For years I had been reading experiences of other Buddhists who faced and overcame life-threatening illnesses. Their moving accounts of fighting against impossible obstacles and facing their fears of death head-on were truly inspirational, but they always seemed far removed from my situation. I had taken health and longevity for granted. It was common for my ancestors to live into their eighties, nineties, or even reach one hundred. But there I was, hanging over a great precipice, saved only by a thread of hope, proclaimed in Nichiren Daishonin's Buddhism, that any illness can be overcome.

Cancer is hell. Cancer is the son of death. In January, 1987 I was 36 years old and in excellent health. My new business venture—a professional resume writing service—had just taken off, and my family life was beautiful. I was living the American dream, in the prime of my life. Quite suddenly I was incapacitated by tremendous back pain, drenching night sweats, insatiable itching all over my body, perpetual low-grade fever, tremor-like chills, and vomiting. I would become so exhausted at work that I would lock the door of my office and sleep under my desk. Both my wife and daughter sensed that I was seriously ill, going out of their way to pamper me and soothe my mind. They saw the concern and fear on my face and were gentle to me.

As the days went by, I became increasingly alarmed by the strange things happening in my body. My eyes' pupils didn't dilate normally, and my skin took on an ashen color. I prayed to dodge the bullet. When the lymph nodes on my neck and behind my right ear swelled up, our family physician immediately ordered a biopsy. That simple procedure was a prelude of the trouble to come. The surgeon, who was taking the biopsy from a swollen lymph node on my neck, nicked my jugular vein, and spent the next half hour trying to stop the bleeding.

The unknown frightened me. Deep inside, I knew that something was terribly wrong. I had been having strange dreams that contained very basic symbolism which I instinctively knew represented danger and death. One evening I dreamed I was driving down a road during the night, when the headlights of the car went off. Feeling out of control and sensing that I was heading for collision, I woke up in panic. Later, I had a dream about an old man who was walking in a garden and was frightened into a heart attack when a kitten jumped out of the brush at a grasshopper. Bolting upright from a deep sleep, I was drenched in sweat. Even if I took just a short, half-hour nap, the sweating was so intense that my clothes and the bedding would be soaked; my perspiration stood on my forearms as if I had been walking in the rain.

The question wasn't *if* there was something drastically wrong with me. Visionary dreams, worsening health, and striking realizations from my Buddhist meditation had already convinced me of that. The question was, "What disease is this?" While engaged in Buddhist meditation or chanting, I tried to focus on overcoming whatever was making me feel so poorly. Like air bubbles rising from the depths of a lake, ideas of danger and dying young came to the surface of my determined prayers. I felt the "fight or flight" reaction switch on within me every few minutes. Not knowing what was actually wrong gripped my every thought with fear and dread. I felt like I was being stalked by an unknown and unseen danger.

Despite my Buddhist training over the previous thirteen years, I could not seem to make any headway into lessening the symptoms of disease that pummeled my body with increasing severity. I was taking nearly a dozen medications. There was powerful pain medication for the debilitating back pain that pounded inside me like Taiko drums, as well as pills for insomnia, itching, muscle relaxation, depression, and more. The pills only made me worse. My wife, Lynn, was convinced that the doctors were poisoning me with so many strong medications, or that the drugs were adversely reacting to each other.

The incident that accelerated the diagnosis occurred after I had taken a shower. I had dried myself and had gotten fully dressed, but when I emerged from the bathroom, I was stricken by a violent chill. My wife and my daughter, Devin, witnessed in shock while my teeth chattered and my whole body shook terribly. I had been having these strong chills for several weeks, but had managed to hide them. My wife called the doctor and pushed him to give us some answers. The possibilities he mentioned were sarcoid, an unknown viral infection, leukemia, or Hodgkin's disease. He did a biopsy and sent it to the Mayo

Clinic. The doctor expected the results in a week, but he said he would try to hurry the clinic. Time moved slowly. After two weeks that felt like six months, I had an answer.

My doctor called late at night and gave me the diagnosis. It was the most sobering telephone conversation of my entire life. My first question was, "How long do I have to live?" His explanation of Hodgkin's disease and what I must do instantly humbled me. I was bitterly disappointed more than I was shocked. Lynn was crying. With 50 milligrams of Halcyon already at work, I was too numb to do much of anything except go to bed and deal with the crisis in the morning. Knowing what was wrong with me was actually a comfort. Now I knew the name of the enemy and its name was cancer.

Almost every person I had ever known who had cancer had died a protracted and painful death. No one in our family that I knew of had ever had cancer. Diseases like cancer happened to other people. Shockwaves spread through my family. Some acted like cancer might be contagious, and some didn't know how to talk to me without sounding as if I was on death row.

I never asked myself the common question, "Why me?" On that night I accepted my diagnosis as a call-to-arms. Rather than look to the heavens and bemoan my miserable fate, I looked within and tried to find the courage to show Lynn and Devin, that I was not afraid. More than a decade of Buddhist training had taught me that disease was a symptom of karma and that it was up to me to create value out of something tragic.

The day after I got the news, I sat down with Lynn and went over the details on how my business was run, and how she had to take over if we were to survive. There were no tears. Lynn is a strong woman of German heritage who understood immediately that we all had different roles to play in defeating the obstacles to come. She would need to run the professional resume business and the household. My daughter would need to grow up quickly, watch over me, and help with chores around the house. My function would be to fight and defeat cancer. Lynn knew that strength, determination, and constant effort in our respective roles would be the only possible way to defeat this enemy.

The morning that I left for the hospital, I sat down with Devin in front of our altar and chanted with her for a few minutes. I then looked deeply into her beautiful green eyes and told her the truth of my condition as far as I knew it, and what I expected from her. Devin did not cry or fuss. She only said, "I'll ask the Gohonzon to make you better, Daddy." As Lynn and I drove the fifty miles to the hospital, nary a word was spoken. Letting me out at the door, she gave me a kiss and went off to work. Because her eyes did not belie her fears, I was able to go into the hospital with the confidence that my family would prevail.

I was admitted to the Hines Veterans' Hospital near Maywood, Illinois, for a diagnostic work-up called "staging," which would determine how far the cancer had spread. It was so gratifying to have someone finally shed some light on my condition and begin administering care. Within a couple of hours a team of doctors saw me. They said that Hodgkin's disease was treatable and if I was going to get cancer, that was the kind of cancer to get. At first, that news was encouraging.

I soon found out that the oncology ward of a large hospital is no place for the fainthearted. During the first 48 hours of my stay, two of my four roommates died before my eyes. Looking at the reality of the cancer ward, I quickly realized how precarious my situation was. All the wonderful principles and theories I had studied for more than a decade were now being actualized before me, and I had now advanced dangerously close to the front lines of suffering, sickness, and death.

The first person whose death I witnessed was a Korean War veteran named Mr. F. He was a thin and feisty man with a terrific sense of humor. After a check-up for an unrelated medical emergency the doctors discovered he had bladder cancer that had spread to his lymph nodes. He had been given a one-in-three chance of survival. I met him a few days after his surgery, and at the time, Mr. F. was in considerable postoperative pain. He was receiving time-release morphine capsules and oxycodone, so his frame of mind was very relaxed.

I watched as he received his first dose of chemotherapy. The oncology nurse brought in a half dozen syringes of varying sizes. The largest looked like a tube of grape juice. Mr. F. was nervous but hopeful that he would beat the cancer. They hooked him up to an intravenous system to deliver the chemotherapy drugs and in twenty minutes he was finished. Ten minutes after receiving chemotherapy, Mr. F. ran to the bathroom and got sick. From my perspective, he seemed to tolerate it very well. But for the rest of the evening he turned on his side towards the wall with a small basin at his side, riding out the effects. All four men in our room went to bed early.

I was sleeping soundly, when around 2:00 A.M., I woke up to a loud crash. Mr. F. had bolted up from bed and knocked his IV against the wall, pulling all the tubes out of his arm. His last words as he looked at me were, "Help, Chuck!" Falling out of bed onto the hard floor, he convulsed, and then went into cardiac arrest. I ran to the nursing station for help, and in less than one minute, two doctors and several nurses were administering CPR to Mr. F., but they couldn't save him. I sat nervously in bed, watching as he made four or five loud snorting sounds, then went limp on the cold tile floor. It was an ugly but relatively short death.

The staff clergyman was summoned from a sound sleep to perform a brief service over Mr. F.'s body, and then he went back to bed. For the clergyman, death was an everyday occurrence, but for me it was a shock. As I witnessed Mr. F.'s crucial moment, I was repelled by the sudden, thrashing horror of it all. The nurses drew the curtain around him and when the coast was clear, I sneaked over to see his body. Perhaps I was driven by some morbid curiosity of death. Mr. F. looked like a statue. His face was in a grimace, and blue. I stared at his body for several minutes, wondering about death, trying to imagine what was going through his mind as he died. I wondered where he was now and what he was feeling.

When his family came an hour later to collect his things, they were in a state of shock. "What the hell happened?" his wife asked. I couldn't offer any information beyond the fact that he fell out of bed and died. I didn't want to give his heartbroken wife and son all the gruesome details. The son gave me a nearly full box of candies that Mr. F. had been snacking on. When they left, I threw it in the trash because I was too superstitious to eat a dead man's food. The next day, a janitor fished it out from the rubbish with a smile.

Oncology professionals see the high drama of life and death played out day and night, yet demonstrate an amazing mixture of compassion and detachment. It might be the only way to retain sanity on a cancer ward. Chemotherapy had been mentioned as the probable treatment for me. I detested the way everyone said "chemo" instead of "chemotherapy." They made the term sound so familiar, so user-friendly. Although I knew very little about chemotherapy, I knew it wasn't user-friendly. It really grated on my nerves when people said "chemo" like they might say "mayo" as in, "Hold the mayo!" The idea of having chemicals with the toxicity of an industrial-strength drain cleaner pumped into my body was not comforting. There was no way I was going to embrace poison as it pumped through my veins. Chemotherapy was serious business. Mr. F. had his first dose and died the same evening.

The very next morning I witnessed the death of Mr. R., a former Chicago policeman who had been admitted the day after I arrived. He was a World War II veteran who was compassionate, but firm. The day he arrived, I introduced him, his two grown children, and his brother to Buddhism and chanting. They were looking for hope anywhere they could find it. A few hours after being admitted, a team of doctors came in and told him that the cancer had spread throughout his body and he might die at any time. Mr. R. didn't show any emotion.

After dinner on the first night, Mr. R. began to burn up with fever and he complained to the nurse of sharp pains in his abdomen and legs. The V. A. hospital wasn't like a private one where the nurses rush in and care for you as if you were at a four-star hotel. He was getting the highest level of care, but there would be no nurses administering nightly sponge baths. He had been examined, fed, he was in a clean bed, and no life-saving medical intervention was needed. I wiped Mr. R. down with a cold compress, and twice lobbied the charge nurse to give him an injection for the pain. Mr. R. kept saying, "Bless you son," as I cooled his fevered, jaundiced body. I tried to encourage him to repeat the words *Nam-myoho-renge-kyo* slowly with me to fight his pain. Even though he didn't understand what the words meant, we repeated them for a few minutes until the morphine put him to sleep.

Later that night, he got up to go to the bathroom, and fell to the floor. Mr. R. was a big man who stood over six feet three inches, and weighed more than 250 pounds. It took several nurses to get him back to bed, but it was obvious to me that he was most embarrassed at his condition, and didn't want to burden the staff or call undue attention to himself. I could see the emotional pain he felt at being helpless. After Mr. R. fell asleep, he seemed to be having bad dreams, as if he was fighting off an unseen enemy. "Go away, please, no," he mumbled. I woke him up and we talked quietly. I got him to chant the mantra a few more times, and he seemed to sleep peacefully for the rest of the night.

The next morning he awoke, smiled at me, and winked. We talked casually until the breakfast cart came in. I looked up from reading and slurping down my corn flakes, to see Mr. R. staring out into space. I called his name, but he just serenely gazed into nowhere. Walking over to him, I looked closely at his eyes, which were fixed and dilated. I waved my hand before his face thinking he was only lost in thought. There was no response. Mr. R. had died with a placid smile on his face.

At his moment of death, Mr. R. was peaceful and dignified. His death was as graceful as falling asleep for a much-needed nap. I was most impressed with the quiet dignity that his body manifested at the final moment, as if he had just heard his favorite song. Could one's brief connection with the Mystic Law of *Nam-myoho-renge-kyo* produce such a startling result? I was shaken to the core of my being. Death and the moment of death were mysterious and thought provoking. Would that person join into the sleep of death with peace and manifest a dignified expression, or would they enter death thrashing and in agonizing pain? The many experiences and writings that I had studied regarding the link between the Mystic Law and its effect on elevating a person's dominant life condition at the moment of death was now being supported by firsthand evidence. I sensed that I was being prepared for a big lesson about the true nature of life and death, in light of my Buddhist studies.

I had little time to mourn my newly fallen friends. Life's compelling demonstration of karmic reward and retribution was a vivid demonstration of the fragile nature of existence. I must have created some very nasty karma to end up as a young man suffering from a deadly cancer that was spreading throughout my body. Another part of my thoughts reflected on how severe reality was for other people. In no way was I unique. There were one hundred beds on my floor alone, with many people ready to die at any moment. Only a few short months before I had been looking to the future and now I wasn't sure that I had one. Life seemed such a paradox. I could do nothing but turn to my beliefs and fight.

From the moment I had fallen ill, I began to repeat *Nam-myoho-renge-kyo* many hours a day, with the hope that I could overcome cancer and live a long, meaningful life. Chanting in the hospital proved to be tricky. I didn't want to invade the privacy of my neighbors. As a Buddhist, it would not have been appropriate for me to go to the hospital chapel and chant my mantra to a cross or statue of Jesus Christ. My best place was the infrequently used patient shower room, where I could chant at whatever volume I liked while staring at a tile wall. When I couldn't chant in the shower room, I just drew the curtains around my bed, sat up straight, Native American style, and chanted in a whisper.

After witnessing two sudden deaths and hearing the groans and screams that occasionally cut through the thin walls and the silence of night throughout the cancer ward, I vowed to chant from dawn to dusk if necessary to change my bad karma into good fortune. Despite the dire prospects that loomed before me, I feared more for Lynn and Devin than I did for myself. The pain that cancer had caused my family filled me with anger and frustration. But it was that primordial soup of unrequited emotion, coupled with the survival instinct, that brought out the warrior within. I vowed to conquer cancer.

LESSONS

Rather than languishing in my sick bed, I took it upon myself to wander the vast cancer ward of Hines Hospital. It was immediately apparent that many people were far sicker than I was. I used my training in faith gained through my thirteen-year association with the American branch of the Buddhist lay organization Soka Gakkai International, to encourage other people. That training included reaching out to others, despite one's own difficult situation. Based on the knowledge that life is eternal, the Bodhisattva gives his or her full energy for the salvation and benefit of others, without regard for his or her own life. Such altruistic attitudes are the desired result of Buddhist practice. To look beyond your own problems and display mercy and compassion for others despite your own difficulties is the epitome of human behavior. It was obvious that such behavior, resulting from years of Buddhist training, would prove invaluable in my personal fight against cancer and how I could influence others to do the same.

Although discouraged by the rapid deterioration of my own health and the somber words of my doctors, I found value in visiting as many patients as I could. Many were old and alone with no family members to bring them comfort. I discovered that the simple act of holding a person's hand in their final moments was more valuable to them than mountains of gold.

One very old man was strapped to the bed, calling out his wife's name at the top of his lungs. He would shout for his beloved "Rose" until the nurses had enough, finally giving him an injection to calm him down and induce sleep. After hearing his plaintive cries for several nights, I asked permission to sit with the old man.

When he looked at me, he seemed surprised that someone other than a nurse or doctor was beside his bed. Turning away, he called out for his wife. I touched his hand and recited *Nam-myoho-renge-kyo* in my most melodious voice. The old man became silent and stared at me in amazement, seeming to really enjoy what I was doing. In my heart I prayed for mercy for this complete stranger. Next I recited a chapter from the *Lotus Sutra* in a slow and rhythmic voice. His face was childlike and awestruck.

I spent only a short time with that veteran, but when I started to leave, despite being restrained, he tried to grab my hand. I took hold of him and looked deeply into his eyes, trying to reassure him that he was not alone. That night the old man was oddly silent. During the night he died. It was a merciful blessing for someone with metastatic prostate cancer.

It seemed as if everyone I met and everything I observed had a purpose. Life was exposing its impermanence to me for the first time with all its beauty and tragedy. But nothing could prepare me for the experience of the fifth night. I had stopped at the TV room to chat with a woman and her daughter. Their loved one, Mr. G., lay moaning loudly in the room directly across from the nursing station. They told me that Mr. G. had bone cancer and there was no possible hope of recovery. They were frustrated because the doctors couldn't do anything to save him or even relieve his intractable pain. They were particularly discouraged because all the clergy could do was tell them God's purpose was not easy to understand. They were offered no hope.

Mr. G. had been hospitalized in isolation for about a month, screaming in agony as the disease progressed. There were no more tears left in either his wife or daughter. He was getting a large injection of morphine every four hours, but the pain continued to worsen. He was in agony during the day, but the night was a living hell. Oddly, I had somehow tuned out this man's sobbing moans. Now that I listened, I could hear the sound of hell in his cries. It was as though he was being hacked to pieces with a machete. I found out that he was a highly decorated World War II hero who had fought in the South Pacific and had been a prisoner of war.

The women were numb with grief and angst as they watched the pillar of their family suffer the greatest protracted agony—a pain so engulfing that it staggered the imagination. I looked in on the man, but after a few moments, had to turn away. Nothing on Earth could ease his pain or restore his sanity. He was begging to die, but was punished by living. The doctors had no idea how much longer he would have to endure. He could die anytime or hang on for another week or so.

I approached the women again and asked if I could tell them about my faith and the power of the Mystic Law to relieve suffering. We spent half an hour talking and I taught them how to chant. The next morning on my way to the cafeteria I bumped into Mr. G.'s wife, who grabbed my arm and said, "Thankfully, my husband died last night, thank you for those words. We had given up. We lost our faith."

The panorama of suffering, hope, and fate that I had witnessed confirmed in my mind the validity of a concept known as the Ten Worlds. For me, death had been something that happened on the highway, or far away in a dimly lit hospital room. Now, everywhere I turned, death was taking someone I had just met. Finding ways to encourage others as their lives hung in the balance seemed to be an art form that wasn't necessarily possessed by doctors, nurses, or clergy. Some of the caregivers had beautiful bedside manner and could truly comfort the sick and dying while others were insensitive, overly blunt, and inconsiderate of emotions and feelings.

Everything seemed to be going wrong with my tests. Every day seemed to bring forth another piece of bad news about how far the cancer had spread. My days were spent going from one test to another. By evening I would be completely exhausted. At night I would sweat and get chills. Loneliness was something I had grown accustomed to over the years.

Lynn and I talked on the phone twice a day. I insisted that she not visit because the trip to the hospital was more than 100 miles, round trip, and I hoped she would ease her mind by con-centrating on the household and business. My other hang-up about visitation was my annoyance with everyone else's visitors. Some men's wives stayed with them from morning until night, never leaving, as if by staring at them long enough, they might get better. The poor, long-suffering women had themselves become patients. It seemed like the longer the women would stay, the more they would be badgered, bullied, and taken for granted by their husbands. After a few weeks of watching those men and their wives, I concluded that men are weaker than women. Most of the men I saw might have been courageous in battle or have been honorable central figures in their homes, but once put into a hospital setting, they turned into whining, complaining, and angry little boys.

Characteristic of my personality, I looked on having visitors supporting me all day as a sign of personal weakness. One part of me would say, "Where is everyone? Doesn't anybody care about me?" The other part of me would say, "I don't want or need any attention, I must handle this alone."

Lynn was as strong as pure titanium I-beams as we dug in for the fight of our lives. She was able to fulfill her responsibilities because of her determined prayer not to be defeated, no matter what. The pressure of the situation built up in Devin, who grew so frustrated and frightened she couldn't concentrate on school. She compensated for her fear and family turmoil by becoming a distraction in her classroom. We were all in the state of hell, but we were calling forth the life condition of Bodhisattva and Buddhahood. The prime point of Buddhism is that karma can be changed through specific actions. Even though it wasn't percep-tible at first, great changes were taking place in all our lives.

VISIONS

It was early March 1987, but for some reason the temperature was about 72 degrees. I had just finished reading Nichiren's writing titled "On the Buddha's Behavior," which details the major persecutions that Nichiren had endured because of his dissemination of his type of Buddhism.[1] Walking down the long hallway to the hospital exit, I kept thinking about Nichiren's courage when he was about to be beheaded. I needed to have that same kind of courage. Feeling most inspired, I decided to go outside to a small grassy area with a few trees about a block away from the hospital. I sat on a bench because the ground was rather moist from melted snow. The bench faced southeast and I proceeded to chant toward the beautiful morning sun. I had not been outside in a week because of the cold weather.

Finishing up about ten minutes of chanting, I recited two prayers from the *Lotus Sutra* as I did every morning and evening, then I continued to fervently chant *Nam-myoho-renge-kyo*. It was nearly 10:00 A.M. My doctors had made their 9 o'clock rounds and mentioned that I would be having a test called the lymphangiogram and I would need special sterile preparations that evening and would be unable to get out of bed. They were not very forthcoming in their explanation of what the procedure would entail.

My heart was heavy with foreboding as I concentrated on chanting. In my mental turmoil, I recalled a passage from the

---

[1] At that time, I was reading an edition of the work that is now out-of-print. This account can be found in "The Actions of the Votary of the *Lotus Sutra*," in the new edition, *The Writings of Nichiren Daishonin* (Tokyo: Soka Gakkai, 1999), pp. 763–782.

Gosho. It simply said that *Myo* was the head, *Ho* the throat, *Ren* the chest, *Ge* the abdomen, and *Kyo* the extremities. As I repeated this idea in my mind, concentrating the sound on my body, one section at a time, I felt an explosion of thrilling energy emerge from deep within, rushing from my chest to my head and cascading down throughout my body. I tried to block out everything except the words melting into their corresponding areas on my body. I shut my eyes and chanted with increasing vigor.

A great glow of amber light appeared in my mind's eye, which caused me to open my physical eyes. I paid no heed to the parking lot or flow of activities that had been there only a moment earlier. My eyes were totally transfixed on the light before me. From the golden rays of the sun, a realistic and highly defined image of the Gohonzon appeared above me. I heard the dramatic sounds of huge drums and soft instrumental music. There were bells, chimes, symbols, and horns perfectly blended into a heavenly music. The volume and soothing nature of the music was like the serenity of a forest lake at dusk beneath an October moon. The uplifting fragrance of flowers and incense heightened my consciousness. I was enveloped and raised to a keen awareness. I was compelled to let go of myself and give in to the vision.

The object I saw was at first about the size of a house door, seeming to undulate like a mirage—coming into sight, then fading out. Hovering in the air, the object seemed to exist between two realities. Part of me was in the world of people, whose eyes see only coarse matter and visions are thought of as meaningless hallucinations or psychosis. The other part of me had entered a dream-like dimension where spirit travel was possible and the sense of vision that could look through any object or see to the ends of the earth. All my senses were at once magnified.

The glowing object was not like the kind of image you see after being exposed to a bright light. In fact, this object was deep ebony, or burnished, black lacquer and looked as real as all the scenery surrounding me. The object began to grow in size. On its surface was Chinese writing in gold that grew in proportion to the object.

I was so enraptured by this vision that I was drawn into the light, completely immersed in pulsing energy. My heart pounded in my chest. My inner spirit then flew out of my body, upward toward the magnificent treasure-tower like an eagle to its nest. Exhilaration fluttered through me. *Nam-myoho-renge-kyo* flowed from my lips as I rode on the winds of rhythmic sound, glorious fragrance, and luxuriant color into the black-and-gold emblazoned tower. By the time I was at the base of the great tower it was of skyscraper proportion. In the aura that radiated from it, I saw huge streamers of vivid red and sharp purple gently rippling to a peaceful wind. The enormous golden Chinese letters on the object transformed before my very eyes into individual Buddhas and entities, representing all the universal aspects of life. There seemed to be hundreds of images, far too many to count. Some were human and looked like the pictures in historical books about Buddhism, and some were not human, but heavenly beings and life forms that I can only describe as God-like in stature. Their radiance was awesome. They were visions of immeasurable purity. There were spiritually advanced beings that seemed to represent a fabulous order of diverse life which I had never imagined possible. Possessing different forms and faces, some were like crystals of holy light, and others appeared as humanoids with multiple arms, legs, and eyes. I looked intensely at their bodies, and they looked completely real to me. Each one seemed to recognize me.

Feeling no fear, only innocent curiosity, I tried to look in their eyes, and as I did, their message appeared in my mind, but I could not understand it. Their images continued to tower above me like Himalayan peaks—mighty, majestic, and imbued with intrinsic power and mercy. On the deepest level, I understood that they were all personifications of *Nam-myoho-renge-kyo*. Each one represented a different aspect and place in the cosmos. Each one praised the Mystic Law. I seemed like a small ember before a giant star. The treasure tower was like a large planet, and its gravity drew me to the surface. Hurtling through space to the center of the object, I now saw only an all-encompassing white light.

When the light had overloaded my senses, I finally knew what the message was. The beings had raised their voices to praise the Mystic Law in all people. Their message spoke to my mind, telling me that I had an important mission. They vowed to protect me.

I felt a tingling glow of energy in my abdomen and especially between my eyes. The sensation was nearly unbearable. Like being thrown back by an electrical shock, I returned to my body and the treasure tower vanished. "What a wonderful dream!" I thought, "Who could believe such a meditation?" I wondered. My awareness returned to the clamor of the hospital grounds' activity. I looked to my right and saw another patient staring at me. He quickly turned away.

After what seemed like a few minutes, I stopped my prayer. Glancing at my watch, I was shocked to see that two hours had transpired. One part of my mind thought that wasn't possible. Another part of my mind quaked in wonder. I began to cry. The tears weren't the kind from physical or mental pain. They were tears of *amrita* that healed the body, mind, and spirit. When I had arrived at the hospital I was a victim. Now, awakened, my heart burned with confidence and determination. It didn't matter whether or not anyone believed that I had such an experience.

I took great solace in the fact that the Buddhist master, Josei Toda, had a similar experience while serving a two-year prison sentence for opposing the Japanese government during World War II. Toda had been under great duress, in a freezing-cold jail cell, when he had the first of two great awakenings. Those experiences gave him the energy and vision to build the foundation for Buddhism's eventual spread to the West and, ultimately, to come into my own awareness. Pride or elation are inferior descriptions of the exaltation I felt inside. Although my ordeal had hardly begun, I already felt a sense of victory.

ENDURANCE

In the evening a nurse came in to sterilize my feet and wrap them with gauze. It seemed no one could really answer my questions about what the doctors were going to do to me. The next morning I was wheeled into an x-ray room, where two surgeons proceeded, with long syringes, to inject blue dye between my toes. The pain was unbelievable. I was gently told to be very still and to not touch my legs even if they itched, which is more difficult than it sounds. I asked permission to softly chant while they proceeded.

I used mantra-powered visualization, imagining my feet as frozen, unable to feel any pain. At first the needle sticks were unbearable, but in a few moments, my mind was able to shut out the pain. Still, I was so nervous that tears started to roll off my cheeks. The surgeons stopped their injections and asked me if I was okay. I told them that I was having a problem blocking out the pain, and kept seeing the faces of my wife and daughter. They asked me if the pain medication was adequate. The staff in my ward had forgotten to give me pain medicine. All hell broke loose as an angry surgeon got on the phone to find out where things had gone wrong. They had been injecting the die between my toes for almost ten minutes with no medication. After that experience, a shot of Demerol and Valium didn't even faze me. For the next twenty minutes, while I was being punctured between the toes, I was able to increase my pain threshold to the point where my body relaxed and I froze out the pain completely.

I lay motionless on the table for several hours. The purpose of the injections between my toes was to expose the lymph node in the top of my foot so that an injection device hooked up to a quart-sized cylinder could then pump blue dye into my lymph system. When an itch happened, I would direct my mind to that place and make it stop. I became quite proficient at this after a while. When my mind attacked one itch, my body would produce another, as if my mind and body were playing games with each other. The final ten minutes of injecting dye into my lymph nodes felt as if someone had thrown gasoline on my legs and set them on fire. When they finished injecting the dye, an x-ray technician took what seemed to be a hundred images of my body from every conceivable angle. The side effects of the procedure made my feet swell up so I couldn't wear shoes, and I urinated blue for a week.

The next day, an irritating resident doctor who was also working on my case paid me a visit. The doctor asked me if I was feeling all right. He then informed me that the radiologist had found a golf-ball-sized tumor pressing into my spine. I was shocked. I told him that a rheumatologist had said that my back trouble was from myofascial pain syndrome. He said that the other doctor was mistaken and, in fact, myofascial pain syndrome was not a scientifically valid condition. He explained it as a catch-all phrase for undiagnosed pain. Further, since the cancer had now affected the bone in my spine, my prognosis was more ominous.

Then he spoke words that drove a spike through my heart. The doctor said that they probably could manage the disease if I could survive the treatment. His manner of speaking seemed to imply that he didn't believe I was up to the task, or that the disease may have progressed too far. I determined to shove my recovery in his face in a few years. I was furious.

Several days later, my primary physician called me into a private room with an oncology support nurse. He told me that I had nodular sclerosing Hodgkin's lymphoma, Stage IV A. The cancer was behind my ear, on both sides of my neck, with diffuse lymph node involvement in my chest and abdomen. The cancer affected my spleen and a huge lymph node tumor was pressing against my spine, eating away the bone. Dr. S. had consent forms for me to sign, authorizing the V. A. to begin aggressive combination chemotherapy. I was encouraged to participate in a clinical trial which would track the results of a control group receiving this therapy. I read the consent forms for MOPP

BAP chemotherapy.[2] Included in the protocol were nitrogen mustard, procarbazine, prednisone, vincristine, adriamycin, and bleomycin. The possible side effects were hair loss, tingling of the extremities, lowered blood counts, bleeding, ulcers, increased levels of blood sugar, increased risk of infection, sterility, demineralization or deterioration of bone mass, heart attack, mouth sores, chemical burns in the blood veins, and the appearance of other cancers. There were dozens of other possible adverse reactions, but I was stuck. My options were to either accept the treatment and risk the perils involved, or die from cancer.

I signed the papers and asked my doctor if he was optimistic. Dr. S. was a quiet but intense man and considered to be the most capable oncologist at Hines. He was assigned to me because I was young and had good potential for surviving. But his response wasn't the reaction I was hoping for. His prognosis was that I had six months to live if the treatment didn't work or if I couldn't tolerate the chemotherapy. He stressed that Hodgkin's disease was now being successfully treated, even with advanced cases like mine.

Dr. S. frankly discussed the irony of cancer. From his experience it was unexplainable why one person responded well to treatment while another person didn't. The human potential was still a mystery to medical science. He was cautiously optimistic in my case because I was physically strong, with no major organ or bone marrow involvement, and I had a strong will to live. But in the same breath, he wanted me to understand that the cancer had

---

[2] "MOPP" and "BAP" are acronyms for the drugs involved in the therapy.

spread extensively and my reaction to treatment wasn't yet known. Although he could offer no guarantees, he emphasized that he would do everything possible to cure me.

That wasn't good enough for me. I asked him if there wasn't something beyond optimism in my case. He looked at me with utmost seriousness and explained that when cancer spreads, all he could offer was optimism. There were too many factors involved, and to be on the safe side, it would be in my best interest to put my affairs in order. He wanted to start chemotherapy that afternoon. I could leave the hospital shortly after the treatment and needed to report back as an outpatient for my second treatment one week later.

It was with great trepidation that I informed Lynn how far the cancer had spread. We had all been hopeful that the cancer would be caught in its earliest stage. There was no way for her to know that I was much worse than she thought. During my staging, I had kept most of the information about the bad test results from Lynn because she had such a heavy burden at home. There would be time enough for serious conversation once I was home. Even I was surprised at how far the cancer had spread.

Despite the bad news, Lynn was very happy that I would be allowed to come home that night. I packed all my belongings right away and waited on my bed in my street clothes for my first treatment. Everyone in my room was happy to see I was going home. They all hoped that they would soon be released to return home instead of being wheeled out to the morgue.

Having an instinctual respect for the power and fury of chemotherapy, I drew the curtains and quietly performed my prayer from the *Lotus Sutra* and chanted *Nam-myoho-renge-kyo* for several hours until it was time to take the medicine. A nurse with a blood pressure kit smiled at me and placed it around my arm, while another nurse prepared my other arm for intravenous delivery of the drugs. Being curious by nature, I asked the nurse why she would be monitoring my blood pressure. She explained that I would receive a test dose of bleomycin and must be carefully observed because that drug had been known to cause heart attack in some people.

Upon that sobering news, I chanted three times and asked the nurse to begin the treatment. The time had come for me to turn poison into medicine. It was time to attack cancer.

CHAPTER 6

Cellular Warfare

My first experience with chemotherapy raised a big red flag of doubt that I could handle the treatment. My nurse said that I might experience a slight metallic taste after the nitrogen mustard and other drugs were administered. I understood that they were poisons that attacked cancer cells as well as healthy cells. Understanding the nature of chemotherapy has no redeeming value beyond knowing that you will soon be feeling very ill. Dispensing the drugs into my system took about twenty minutes. I just lay on the bed, trying to feel something happening in my body. For one brief moment, I thought that I might breeze right through the treatment. That's when I got my first taste of nitrogen mustard in action. There are probably cancer drugs with similar or greater effects, but I pray that I never have to experience any of them. Nitrogen mustard turned me inside out with nausea and vomiting. None of the other drugs were quite as ruthless in attacking my body.

After thirty minutes of vomiting, I grabbed some sick bags and went to meet my wife downstairs. Every minute or two, an uncontrollable wave of nausea would stop me. I made it downstairs and waited in a corner, watching for my family, and heaving into a bag. We had no opportunity to rejoice about my release from the hospital after my month-long stay.

I was scheduled for six cycles, twice monthly, of aggressive combination chemotherapy, and faced the possibility of four more cycles if the disease wasn't expunged from my body within six months. My clinical trial also called for randomized selection for radiation therapy right after the chemotherapy. If I survived, the clinical trial would keep track of my progress over the next ten years.

I was really hoping that I would be one of the lucky ones, take my chemotherapy, and walk out as if I had received a common flu shot. The sessions when I received nitrogen mustard turned into a waking nightmare. After the first administration of that agent, I could smell its odious stench through its plastic chamber on the other side of the room. Even with all my chanting I could not stop the problems in my stomach. I took some consolation from the fact that nitrogen mustard was derived from mustard gas developed by the Germans for chemical warfare because of its extremely irritating, blistering, and disabling effects. As a pacifist, I found it wonderfully ironic that a substance created to kill or harm was now being used to heal.

The day after my first treatment, I was shocked when I looked in the mirror. My face was moon-shaped in appearance, all round and puffed out. I went home with a half dozen bottles of pills that comprised the oral medications that were part of the Southwest Oncology Group 7808 protocol. Lynn got me organized with a computer printout that enabled me to keep track of taking the medications at the right time. There were few problems that week except for increasing pain in the arm where the chemotherapy drugs had been administered. By the time of the second phase of the first cycle, my arm felt like someone had poured caustic acid on it. That was the beginning of a seemingly never-ending supply of painkillers. By the second treatment my whole body was experiencing pain.

For some inexplicable reason—even the oncology staff was amazed—my second phase of chemotherapy produced no nausea. I sat down, received the treatment, and half an hour later I drove home as if I had been injected with saline solution. However, it was not long before the progressive nature of my chemotherapy began to erode my quality of life to the point that I wanted to quit. My strong determination met face to face with my inner coward—a voice that would tell me to kill myself and avoid the suffering.

For the first several months, I had to consciously override and drown out the inner coward with my chanting. In retrospect, I can now clearly see that the inner coward has many manifestations. It takes the form of self-doubt, guilt, self-pity, remorse, escapism, and self-destructive urges. At the time when I was fending off the devilish voice, I thought I might be going insane from all the drugs and the pressure. The inner coward would speak in a sinister whisper, "Your family has suffered enough, you'll never make it, why don't you drive the car into a big oak tree. Oh, that would be too messy. Why don't you hang yourself in the stairwell?" The inner coward is nothing more than the fundamental darkness that is inherent in human life.

CORNERED

Cancer is a ravenous monster that backs you up against death's door. Within a few months, we were on the verge of bankruptcy, and the Internal Revenue Service was threatening us with seizure of what little assets we had. I had nowhere to run or hide. As far as my material possessions were concerned I could not have cared less. I worried only about my family. The IRS could take everything if they had to, but they couldn't take my life. In my heart there was no false attachment to material things, but there was no way that I wanted the IRS to come and disrupt our life. Lynn and Devin were strong, but they didn't need to find out how to live with nothing but the shirts on their back, especially not now. Still, the inner coward would speak up, trying to break our fighting spirit. My wife and daughter were also plagued by their own inner cowards.

We were under siege. Adding to our obstacles, my father-in-law suffered what was first thought to be a heart attack and was hospitalized. Now Lynn had to divide even more of her time between two households, trying to support everyone and hold everything together. Devin could not understand why both her father and grandfather had to suffer so much, let alone at the same time.

It became crystal clear to us that we couldn't escape our karma, and it was closing in on us daily. We had no choice but to continue chanting *Nam-myoho-renge-kyo*, no matter how badly we felt. One of our Buddhist friends encouraged Lynn by saying that despite our suffering now, the outcome would strengthen our characters and result in something positive. Our friend insisted that when we finally overcame all our difficulties, we would be able to look back at this period in our life together and feel a tremendous sense of appreciation, because we were able to defeat every obstacle, turning each problem into a golden memory.

It was no small task gaining the upper hand on my weakness. Each day I felt poorly, as if I had consumed large quantities of hard liquor and now had to suffer the inevitable hangover. I had a tingling sensation in my hands and feet, 24 hours a day, as though waves of electricity were shooting from one appendage to another. At the same time, my hands and feet were so numb that I could not feel my toes or the bottom of my feet, nor could I feel the tips of my fingers. I started the treatments with a nice head of brown hair, which fell out in clumps, later growing back silver-gray and white, as if I had suffered a terrible fright.

I was experiencing acute panic attacks that made me feel as if I was on the verge of a seizure and the top of my head was going to blow off. The fatigue became so overwhelming that a simple task like washing the dinner dishes was a big challenge that would leave me thoroughly exhausted for hours. As the pills and the treatments continued, my nausea would appear at any time and linger indefinitely. Some of my favorite foods became loathsome to smell, let alone eat. I was given pills, suppositories, and injections for nausea, but after the third cycle of chemotherapy, nothing worked.

Off the record, my doctor advised me to try marijuana, which quickly stopped all nausea except for that experienced on treatment days. The interesting thing about using marijuana as an anti-nausea agent was the fact that it was legal in Illinois to prescribe it as a medicinal drug, but it could not be obtained legally through a pharmacy! The prescription drug Compazine that I had been given was utterly useless in my case. In me, it caused a psychotic side effect of panic attacks that were very frightening.

I had no idea that marijuana was useful for nausea and stimulating the appetite. I thought it was nothing more than a recreational drug. I was wrong. As a medication, marijuana was far superior to any of the pharmaceuticals that I was being given. Its results were instantaneous, and the dosage could be controlled. It was infuriating that just because of politics, I was forced into the black market in order to secure a legal medicine, when I was so sick and weak that I could barely walk a city block without keeling over.

Every day, my arms throbbed with excruciating pain caused by the chemotherapy drugs. My veins hardened like stone and could be rolled around like plastic tubes. It was nearly impossible for me to lift my arms over my head or pick up anything because the pain was so severe. My fingertips were so numb that I nearly had a nervous breakdown in the supermarket from just trying to separate some thin plastic bags for our vegetables. I couldn't feel the bags. I was panicked and ashamed, unable to solve the problem. I felt like crying because I had become so damn helpless.

PROGRESS

For more than three months after my treatment began, I would wake up at sunrise and chant from my bed, gripped in a seemingly never-ending fight with my illness. Later in the day, I would sit in my chair chanting and reading the writings of Nichiren. One of the most meaningful passages I took to heart was his encouragement to the parents of a small child who had become gravely ill. "*Nam-myoho-renge-kyo* is like the roar of a lion. What sickness can therefore be an obstacle?"[1] In my agony, I sought to make that verse my motto in fighting the onslaught of cancer, treatment, and financial devastation. My faith was being challenged by forces that were so overwhelming that the inner coward was delighted.

The depth of my negative karma was obvious. As I looked back on my 36 years on Earth, I was hard-pressed for a reason why I was receiving so many negative effects in my life. Before I got cancer, my conduct had been both good and bad. But in my heart, I felt I had been a decent, hard-working, and spiritually-minded person who was working on improving himself. After some serious self-reflection I understood that if my past sins or misconduct as a young man produced the horrors I was now experiencing, then all the prisons in the world would be cancer wards and two-thirds of the world's population would be on their death beds. I reflected on why good people are often laid to waste in violence, disaster, or by illness, while seemingly evil and corrupt people often live long and stable lives. The key to the paradox is the inescapable law of karma. What doesn't show up in one life will surely appear in the life to follow.

Fighting cancer, enduring the rigors of chemotherapy, and fending off imminent financial disaster was a heavy load to

---

[1] Nichiren Daishonin, *The Writings of Nichiren Daishonin* (Tokyo: Soka Gakkai, 1999), p. 412.

carry. With each passing day, I was challenged with the opportunity of moving forward or giving in to defeat. I looked for inspiration and strength in my faith. I studied and chanted as much as my strength and willpower would allow me. Even though Devin was so young, she would sit before our altar and pray for me every day.

One morning, while we were having breakfast together before Devin went off to school, she told me that she had a dream about me the previous night. In her dream I had died and she walked with all her classmates by my casket at the funeral. I nearly choked on my toast. It was at that moment I knew that the pressure of this whole ordeal was getting to be too much for everyone and we needed a big breakthrough. I assured my daughter that people dream all kinds of things and most of them never come true. She didn't believe me. I knew I was getting better despite the obvious signs of physical deterioration, but that meant nothing to a child who saw her father getting weaker by the day.

Despite the debilitating complications of chemotherapy, it appeared that the cancer was responding to treatment. Dr. S. was very encouraged to see the lymph nodes shrinking in size. He was now quite familiar with my practice of Buddhism and told me to keep chanting. Despite feeling incredibly weak, I was holding up well under the torturous treatment. There was no complete remission yet, but something wonderful was happening inside me.

The reason that the tides seemed to be turning was because I had been using the mantra-powered visualization on a daily basis. After my spiritual awakening in March, I had researched the subject of Buddhist visualization for healing, and was astonished to find that many people had used it successfully.

It was uplifting to read about so many people with terminal disease who had successfully employed chanting, visualization, and guided imagery when medical science had reached its limit. Evidence from Japan and other parts of the world showed that life was frequently restored, improved, or peacefully ended. I found pride in possessing a viable method of body/mind healing. With the excellence of medical science and my visualization, anything was possible. Even in the face of death, which could happen at any moment, I felt confident in my faith and my future afterlife.

Five years earlier, I had had the opportunity to witness the death of a Japanese woman, Mrs. C., who had sincerely practiced Buddhism for 30 years. In 1979, she was diagnosed with breast cancer and underwent chemotherapy. We were overjoyed when she went into remission. At that time, her daughter was seventeen and her son was ten. Because she was a widow, if she had died at that time, her children's ability to live independently would have been in question. They had no relatives who could assume guardianship, so they would have become wards of the state. Shortly after her daughter turned 18, Mrs. C.'s cancer recurred with a fury, and she was again hospitalized. She had been in the hospital only a few days when I was informed that she had fallen into a coma. When her daughter and I arrived, she was lying very still. We started to chant and when she heard her daughter's voice she began to thrash around in bed in a struggle to wake up. She calmed down when her daughter stroked her head and told her everything was all right.

Within two hours, about ten people had come into her room and joined in chanting for her. Elsewhere, at a fellow Buddhist's home, Lynn and Mrs. C's eleven-year-old son were chanting together with others. I had never seen anyone in the final stages of cancer, nor had I ever witnessed a person on their deathbed. I prayed for her with all my might.

Before long, her eyes opened up and peered directly forward as if she was witnessing some great spectacle. Her arms lost their rigidity, gently sliding down her side and going limp. Her face was peaceful, and her cheeks a rosy hue. I believe that I witnessed Mrs. C. reach enlightenment. Moved beyond words, I had no idea her courageous struggle and dignity would be a model for me only six years later.

On a daily basis, I used mantra-powered visualization to fight the unseen but ever-present enemy. In this process, my determined inner voice would first say, "Brain. Thank you very much. Your masterful work, keeping all the systems harmonized, is wonderful. Brain! I implore you, unless you wish your existence to cease, you must send your magnificent healing chemicals in the proper amounts to our problem areas at once."

I would take the same approach with my heart, liver, lungs, kidneys, stomach, muscles, bones, and all the integrated systems of my body. I would congratulate my lungs for their great effort, and praise my heart for beating with such perfect rhythm. I became fascinated with anatomy and could really see, visit, and experience each organ or system. My reality-based consciousness, merged with the collective unconscious, moved through my body like a warrior on a microscopic battlefield. While chanting, I would imagine glorious, holy light penetrating the areas where there was disease.

I knew that many people had used the same basic techniques and produced spectacular results. Despite my enthusiasm there was a battalion of obstacles dead ahead.

THE WALL

Perhaps the most serious aspect of my cancer and the litmus test of mantra-powered visualization was the lymph node tumor that was pressing against the third vertebra of my spine. In 1985, before I was diagnosed with Hodgkin's lymphoma, I was experiencing serious back pain and was sent to a rheumatologist for diagnosis and treatment. The remedy was electrical and ultrasound stimulation, and the application of hot packs, which got me back on my feet again.

In late 1986, I was again stricken with back pain so strong that I was taken to the emergency room, and referred back to the rheumatologist. This time the pain was completely out of control, interfering with my sleep cycle and bending my frame over.

After another complete diagnostic work up, I was given more of the same kind of treatment, but this time it didn't work. I was taking strong medicine for pain and muscle relaxation, as well as ultrasound treatment three times a week. After a month of increasing agony, my Korean doctor recommended acupuncture. I had read many articles and heard the experts argue whether or not acupuncture was a legitimate therapy or if the results were produced by the patient's prior inclination to believe. I was aware of the power of suggestion, but I wanted to see proof. I trusted my doctor and had no positive or negative opinion about acupuncture. I didn't know what to believe. I just wanted to get out of the severe pain that conventional treatment couldn't quell. Acupuncture was painless and two weeks later my back felt normal again. When acupuncture stopped my pain, all the other cancer symptoms appeared at once; it was like being jumped in an alley by a half dozen thugs.

Immediately prior to my final diagnosis in the V. A. Hospital, a team of doctors making their rounds came into my room. The chief of oncology asked me questions. He wanted to know if I was still having back pain. When I responded that acupuncture had stopped the pain, he shook his head in disbelief. Seven years later, we spoke of my case during a chance meeting at the V. A. He remembered me. His first comment after shaking my hand and patting me on the back was to say, "You were the one with the big tumor on your spine that disappeared." He was from India, and I was surprised when he gave me a look of disbelief when I mentioned acupuncture seven years earlier.

At the time, I wasn't even aware that I had a tumor in my back. It was most discouraging to learn that the tumor had eaten an eighth of an inch of one vertebra. It was a big let-down to discover that the cancer could possibly paralyze me, or spread throughout my bones at any time. For the next six months, I used visualization to first shrink and kill the tumor, and then begin reconstruction of the bone mass at the third lumbar vertebra.

In my case, the results were gradual. Every day I tried to make headway, despite fatigue and feeling poorly. I felt my best when I was actively utilizing mantra-powered visualization. In four months I had experienced excellent progress in shrinking the tumors on my neck. What was happening deeper inside my body, only a CT scan would tell.

One of the most frustrating aspects of chemotherapy was the drop in my blood counts. Fatigue was overwhelming. I faced the third cycle of chemotherapy with unfathomable dread. By that time, I would become violently ill on the way to the treatment. The mere thought of impending treatment would evoke the smell of nitrogen mustard and I would feel nauseated. The chemotherapy nurses were exceptionally patient, considerate, and kind, despite the sight of a grown man struggling with psychosomatic nausea. I would receive huge injections of anti-nausea medicine, to no avail. The third cycle of chemotherapy had me totally shaken.

On treatment days, my mind felt like it had split in two. The intellectual part knew that the treatment was ultimately bearable and I would be partially knocked out and would vomit for the next seven or eight hours. If one really thinks about it, there are countless things in life worse than chemotherapy. Any parent who has lost a child, or a burn victim can attest to the life condition of hell. I knew from the viewpoint of the Ten Worlds that I would be descending into hell, taking with me my mutually possessed state of Buddhahood. The other part of me didn't want to feel the pain because it knew already how much suffering was involved.

That day of my third treatment, I almost had a nervous breakdown during my pre-chemotherapy exam with Dr. S. He arranged an immediate appointment with a counselor. My treatment would begin later that afternoon after all the blood chemistry results were analyzed.

The counselor listened carefully to my tale of woe. So much pent-up frustration over my finances and health came to the surface that I started sobbing. In mid-sob I understood the problem without the counselor saying anything. I was human and afraid. Courage could defeat fear. There wasn't anything the counselor could say that I didn't already know about solving my problems. Winning was up to the individual. I stopped the session and told the doctor that I knew it was all up to me, thanking him profusely for just listening.

Lynn and I went into the chemotherapy room somewhat stronger than before. When the treatment time got closer, the inner coward raised its ugly head once again and I began to shake like a leaf. Tears filled my eyes as they began the IV administration. Lynn looked me in the eye, challenging me with a look that said, "Be a man, now." I mustered up my courage and started chanting to myself. As soon as they began, I began to get sick. It took twice as long to finish the treatment because I was so violently ill.

Some schools of psychosomatic healing or new age healing believe that, in the case of chemotherapy, the mind should embrace the drug because of its healing powers. Instead of hating chemotherapy, they believe that one should open the body to its healing power. In my case, I hated chemotherapy and no mental discipline would ever change that fact. I did not open my body or spirit to it, nor did I welcome it. I wanted it out of my life as soon as possible. The idea that if the disease wasn't wiped out of my body, another four treatments would be required made my chanting all the stronger. I prayed fervently that the chemotherapy would end with the sixth cycle and I would never have to experience it again. It doesn't take long to gain a mountain-sized, negative respect for the power of chemotherapy.

With chemotherapy comes the likelihood that the person will be plunged into the state of hell for much of the treatment. Anyone who has gone through aggressive chemotherapy and beat cancer has just received a medal from the universe. The hell of chemotherapy is often a gift of life. I see no benefit in trying to embrace a wild panther, a ruthless killer. It is better to concentrate on surviving the fury. If someone can force him- or herself to embrace that, more power to them. I don't believe there is the slightest benefit from embracing chemotherapy. But if chemotherapy can help, you must have the *courage* not to run from it. Just pray for strength and courage, and ride out the storm.

Finally the treatment was finished, but I was unable to walk, and had to be wheeled out to the car. Lying on the back seat of our car, I was hardly able to move and was fighting to remain conscious. I was afraid that if I blacked out, that I would choke to death on my own vomit. I was violently ill all the way home. I don't know how Lynn managed to drive without breaking down emotionally on that ride home. The only thing that kept me conscious was prayer. My body was on autopilot, in survival mode. In my prayers I tried to visualize the inside of my body as turbulent seas that were turning into gentle waters. Lynn somehow managed to get us home, and got Devin to help her drag me into the apartment. I closed myself in the bedroom, still semiconscious, fighting never-ending waves of nausea. It took seven hours to reach the end of that major assault. It may sound overzealous, but at my regular time of 7 P.M., I pulled myself out of bed, faced east, and recited the first of my twice-daily prayers from the *Lotus Sutra: The Liturgy of the Buddhism of Nichiren Daishonin.* It took me about thirty or so minutes to finish, compared to my usual time of twenty minutes. That action brought back my concentration and my nausea lessened. Within an hour, my nausea reduced to four times an hour instead of being constant. By that time I no longer felt drugged, just sick. Chanting had truly brought me through the worst.

During the entire course of my treatment, I sought the encouragement and advice of others. One of the most important people that advised me during the ordeal was a Japanese business executive and Buddhist friend, Mr. S. At every opportunity, Mr. S. and his wife would encourage us to continue fighting so we could give hope to other people who were suffering. "Everyone is watching you . . . your behavior," he said. "You're showing everyone the power of the Mystic Law," he went on. He would encourage me every time we met, and his frequent calls were a lifeline.

There were other people of my faith who took up our battle as their own. Mrs. E., a Japanese woman, would call me up during the day, and if I sounded weak or depressed to her, she would shout, "Come on, Chuck! Wake up! You've got to get strong! Get up and chant!" It was like having my own private drill sergeant and I really appreciated her pushing me to fight. Another Japanese woman I knew who had moved to Florida sent word that she was chanting two hours a day for my health. It would not be possible to fully express my gratitude for all my Buddhist and non-Buddhist friends who sent their prayers and gave us encouragement.

Each treatment took a little bit more out of me. After the second phase of the third cycle, I felt as if I had reached the end of my physical and mental strength. I had reached the "wall" described by long distance runners when they come to a point in the race where all their physical and mental energy seems stymied. If you don't get past the wall, you will be defeated. Mrs. E. pushed me right through the wall.

The fourth series of treatments was about to commence. This time I had my wits about me. Dr. S. had gone on vacation to England, and a brilliant young oncologist, Dr. M., would be handling my treatment. This time there were no tears, just stiff determination to meet this battle head on. I used mantra-powered visualization to navigate the rough seas of nausea. I was again reduced to a stupor. In my semiconscious state, I tried to hold on to the image of stretching my arms out to calm the waters. The treatment turned out to be no more severe than the last one. Knowing what to expect, I tried to repeat my strategy of using the evening recitation of the *Lotus Sutra* to break the rising tide of sickness. After surviving that fury, the cumulative effects of the treatment began to rapidly break down my strength and blood counts.

CHAPTER 7

Into the Bardos and Back to Earth

I n July 1987, because of a compromised immune system weakened by chemotherapy, I became very ill from a urinary tract infection. Confined to bed at home, my fever skyrocketed to 104 degrees for several days. I was too sick to begin my fifth cycle of chemotherapy. After getting advice from our oncology nurse, I was immediately hospitalized and put into an isolation room. A team of doctors evaluated me to determine what was wrong and how to bring my fever under control.

Our whole world looked as if it were crumbling down. Both Lynn and I knew that the crucial moment had come. I was having strange dreams about my dead grandparents. I sensed death, though not in a bad way. My sense of death felt like being near a great ocean, hearing the waves, smelling the air. The fear of death that had gripped me immediately after my diagnosis, was reconciled during my mystical experience back in March.

Being human, I was afraid for my family. Seeing the grotesque nature of cancer, I was afraid to experience those agonies but was confident from my faith that I would end my life victoriously. When I first looked at the reality of my own mortality, I doubted that I had accomplished much in my lifetime. The further I got into my struggle against cancer, the more I realized that my behavior was now an example for others on how to fight their own battle against disease.

When death comes knocking on the door, people bargain with the gods. I had staked my adult life on Buddhism and would see it through to the end, no matter what. Bargaining with the ultimate spiritual reality of the universe, I vowed: "If I overcome cancer, I'll tell my story far and wide!" Death looked easy, but dying seemed hard. After having what some would call a near-death experience and others would call a trip into the *bardos*, I made the determination to live.

In recent years, much attention has been paid to near-death experiences. People who were pronounced clinically dead and those under great duress have documented their experiences of separating from their body and traveling through a tunnel toward a great light. Firsthand accounts and anecdotal data of life after death are as old as civilization. Certain scientists have attributed this universal experience to a chemical reaction in the brain when oxygen is cut off or the blood flow is impaired. Science can prove that similar results may be obtained in a clinical setting. But there is much more to near-death experiences than chemical reactions in the human brain. The eternity of life cannot be validated through a controlled experiment.

In Betty Eadies' account of her near-death experience,[1] she tells of meeting loved ones, traveling through a tunnel of light, meeting Jesus, having all of her questions answered, and being shown around heaven. Her account of the afterlife is filled with Christian imagery, and it portrays a kinder and gentler afterlife than that of fundamentalists. When reading about other near-death experiences, one might come to believe that after dying, separating from the body, traveling through the tunnel and into the light, that the experience is complete.

I wondered why Eadie's experience of death was so different from the one I had in July 1987. Near-death experiences have many things in common. People separate and hover over their bodies, encounter a tunnel of light and meet relatives or important religious figures from their lives. What happens after death is pure speculation unless you have experienced it for yourself. My own father believed "When you're dead, you're dead."

After much inner debate, I have decided to describe in this book my boomerang through the afterlife, in order to expound on the greatness of life and the universe. The difficulty of describing the near-death experience is lack of adequate language concepts with which to convey ideas of a transcendental world beyond our reality-based concepts of space and time. Metaphor and analogy are probably the most effective way of describing the dynamic of the afterlife.

---

[1] See Betty Eadie, Curtis Taylor (contributor) and Melvin Morse, *Embraced by the Light* (New York: Bantam, 1994).

Recalling my envelopment into the realm *Ku*, or the non-local state of existence and non-existence, I have emerged with some observations. Life after death defies all definitive or absolute description because it is completely subjective. Death isn't the end nor is it a place to go. The dimensions of death and life exist al' around us, permeating all phenomena. Heaven is not in the sky and hell is not below the earth. The actual secret of death is found in the continuing life moment. Like waves on the ocean, life rises up, and falls in an unbroken pattern on the sea of eternity. One of the fears we may have of death is annihilation of consciousness. Like wafting smoke, we rise up and are absorbed by the atmosphere. In death, you become everywhere.

When death comes, you are stripped of your worldly possessions, pride, vanity, status, and ego. Position, wealth, and social standing are as meaningless as play money at your local bank. The only thing that you take with you is the accumulated treasures of your heart and the record of your karma. Everything you have thought, spoken, or done is permanently recorded in your life. Your fundamental life entity, inseparably encompassed in a sphere of karma, embarks upon the journey of death. Whatever you were is left behind. The personality as we know it is a temporal assimilation and has no relevance, but your intrinsic nature is evident and endures throughout space and time.

On the second night of my hospitalization, I was still racked by fever and feeling very miserable. A resident doctor had tried to administer ampicillin but I refused the drug because I was allergic to penicillin. I fought with myself to keep chanting. I was so tired.

I woke up at 3:45 A.M. with a start. A numbing, sparkling, bluish-black force surrounded me and I felt like I was being swallowed up into a vortex. Automatically, I chanted *Nam-myoho-renge-kyo* and thought loudly, "Let me win or die now!" After blacking out momentarily, I became aware again and found myself chanting in a void blacker than the darkest India ink, a place completely devoid of light. In the next instant, the absolute blackness around me exploded into a translucent, twilight blue.

Floating above my body, I heard what sounded like a loud, high-pitched bell, and I heard and felt a loud popping sound. A large tunnel of light, much larger than my room, appeared out of nowhere, obscuring the sight of my physical surroundings. This light was awesome and compelling to the degree that it was impossible to resist. My being was white and golden light, possessing an energetic form, rather than flesh, the five senses, and my conscious mind. Instantaneously, I saw a multitude of magnificent spiritual beings of incredible stature and compassion who appeared from the light, approaching me at great speed with arms extended.

I could not move forward into the light or anywhere. I hovered there at the base of the great vortex with my vision transfixed on the multitude of beings approaching me. Beneath me and around me I sensed evil and danger. When the assembly was upon me, the sensation of evil vanished. I recognized this host at once as a gathering of mighty buddhas, whom I had honored with my life. A force drew us into the tunnel toward the origin of the light. A kaleidoscopic history of the universe and the dimensions of life revealed itself on the tunnel walls.

Beholding all the images, I realized that I had repeated this familiar journey countless times before. My life was throbbing with ecstasy and love, trillions of times more wonderful than seeing your true love after a great absence. I was guided, protected, and spiritually enjoined by familiar beings who sped my way into a spectacular realm of tranquil light.

I had no sense of time or distance. The death experience might be understood as similar to blending in with everything inside and around you. I could be at the farthest corner of the most distant galaxy in just one thought. The entire universe fit on the head of a pin. You don't become aware of what is transpiring so much as you become awareness itself. Moving into the source of an all-encompassing light of incalculable vastness and beauty, my spirit was synchronous with the vibration of *Nam-myoho-renge-kyo* that took the form of light and sound. The light originated from sound and the sound reverberated with the light. At that moment, I realized that getting off the Wheel of Samsara—escaping the perpetual cycle of birth and death replete with all the joy and suffering it entails—is an illusion of consciousness. You *are* the wheel.

The exotic fragrance of sandalwood filled my senses and the realm reverberated with the vibration of *Nam-myoho-renge-kyo*. I was a baby reunited with his mother, a drop of water returning to the ocean, a speck of dust falling back to earth. I was part of a great spiritual reality that drew me into its bosom. There had never been anything separating us. Full awareness swept over me. I was not a soul or personality, but an integral part of something infinitely greater and holy. My true entity, free of all impediments, moved toward the light like a sperm to the egg.

My afterlife experience was not a walk into quiet meadows or reuniting with deceased loved ones. I was in the presence of great beings of the light who lived and died throughout the universe, sowing the seeds of enlightenment wherever they went. Their honors and blessings were psychically evident, radiating glory like twin suns in the dark of space. Those enlightened entities were not permanent residents of the afterlife, but existed there like blood cells passing through the human heart before flowing through the rest of the body. The afterlife is not an astral warehouse for the dead. I perceived it to be the origin of consciousness and energy. All life and matter in the entire universe is one vast entity. I was made aware that life is prevalent everywhere in the universe and myriad realms, with countless worlds that do not conform to our conception of environments suitable for the life as we know it.

Although I am not a scientist, I discovered that what we perceive as our universe is not the only universe. My observation of the "known" universe was that it is akin to one cherry among a bunch of cherries on a tree, in an orchard that continues indefinitely. The quantum world is a bardo of actuality and potential, moving to a cosmic law of nonlocal physics that requires both mystic wisdom and science in order to penetrate its secrets. It was obvious that there are quarks, atoms, planets, solar systems, galaxies, small, medium and major world systems, dark matter, and the totality of our conception of the physical universe, but the scale from micro to macro is without beginning or end. There is no singular point of creation because life and the universe are eternal, repeating a cycle that has no beginning or end. What appears as the beginning or creation, such as the big bang, is the phase that follows destruction that

121

repeats the eternal cycle of formation, development, decline, and extinction. Furthermore, it was obvious that new universes were being born and dying constantly. Pulsing at the core of eternity, the universe, and the myriad forms of manifest life is *Nam-myoho-renge-kyo*, or the singular moment of beginningless time.

In a billionth of a microsecond I fused with the light. I felt like a small boy finding his mother after being lost. There was no fear, only love, mercy, and indescribable fulfillment. I was on center stage with countless life forms and we were all part of the greater life. We were like probes returning to the home base to report our findings. I realized at once that what exists in the light is the merciful, loving parent, and we are its child.

The purpose of this book is healing. What I experienced in the afterlife is far beyond the scope of this writing and deserves its own full account. However, it is worthy of mention, to affirm that in the process of death, one truly does review one's own life in all its detail. That karmic review of one's true entity does not end with the life just experienced, but encompasses all previous incarnations as well.

When I had reached the zenith of my experience, a voice emerged from within me and said, "There is more to do, return." At that moment, the light intensified and I awoke back into my pain-filled body and the drab isolation room. I blinked my eyes to adjust to the light. I noticed that it was 3:48 A.M., the exact time I had been born. My body temperature felt normal as if my fever had broken. Tears rolled down my cheeks without pause. I drank a glass of cool water and toasted life. In my heart, I knew that I had overcome cancer.

HOMEWARD BOUND

Two days after my near-death experience I had a CT scan to find out what was going on in my body. For the first time since my battle with cancer began, I felt that I was now healed and cancer free. The swelling of the lymph nodes on my neck and behind my ear had disappeared, and the doctors could find no other enlarged lymph nodes. The opinion of Dr. S. was that if the lymph nodes on the surface were shrinking, then the ones on the inside should also be responding. The only way to know for sure was with a CT scan.

Two days after the CT scan, a team of doctors came through my partially-closed door, surprising me. I was deeply involved in chanting, with tears streaming down my cheeks. They thought I was upset. Dr. B. calmed me down and said that she had some very good news. The CT scan results had come in and the x-rays showed I was now cancer free. When they left, I paced up and down the halls, all over the ward, saying "Hello" to every person I saw. Lynn was ecstatic on hearing the good news. The pressures of running our business, raising our daughter, and dealing with a dying loved one had been monumental.

Dr. B., the second-in-command for oncology at Hines V. A., was personally handling my care while Dr. S. vacationed in England. I was expected to remain in the hospital for at least two more weeks until my blood counts elevated to acceptable levels. I used that time to minister to the other cancer patients. I visited with them, listened to their problems, offered encouragement, and tried to teach chanting to those who were willing. In many cases, my efforts to get others to try chanting were futile. Most were already set in their ways and were unwilling to try Buddhist prayer and visualization. I became very frustrated after seeing dozens of people who had left their fate up to their doctors and God, somehow not seeing the need for their own spiritual efforts. Sobered and saddened at the never-ending spectacle of suffering on the cancer ward and my apparent inability to motivate more patients, I just wanted to get out of the hospital as soon as possible.

However, I was reminded of the Mystic Law's tremendous mercy and power when I visited Mr. Z., who was in the isolation room next to mine. He had advanced cancer of some kind, had taken a turn for the worse, and was unable to move a muscle. He just lay in bed, propped up and motionless, fitted with an oxygen mask, and fully conscious of his decline. He waited for death to take him. Mr. Z. could not speak and could only move his eyes. I sat with Mr. Z. several times over a two-day period, keeping him company, and trying to bring a little joy into his very difficult world. I told Mr. Z. that he had nothing to worry about. I taught him how to chant using the inner voice and told him he could release himself. I told him that prayer would help him along the way, and that there was nothing to fear. The last time I saw Mr. Z.—when I got up to leave—a tear ran down his cheek. I told him everything would be great and to hold onto his prayers and look for the heavenly light. That night, Mr. Z. passed away in his sleep.

After I was in the hospital for one full week, I learned from Doctor B. that it would take a minimum of five more days for my body to reach the required blood count levels that would allow me to safely leave the hospital. Due to my weakened immune system, being sent home too early would risk my having to return to the hospital with serious complications. The doctors said that I might not be so lucky the next time.

ACTUAL PROOF

It dawned on me that mantra-powered visualization could be used to raise my blood counts on command. With great determination, I told Dr. B. of my plan, and that I would be going home in two days. Dr. B. was a grand Indian woman of knowledge, dignity, and compassion. Being Hindu, culturally sophisticated, and well-versed in India's rich spiritual traditions, she totally understood the purpose of my Buddhist practice and what I wanted to do by focusing my mind's energies on my blood counts. She laughed and said, "If anyone can do this, it is you Mr. Atkins." I had no doubt, either.

The isolation room had been like a crypt before. Now it was one of only a handful of private rooms on the ward. Being close to the nursing station, the isolation room represented the most critical cases. It was an environment I wanted to change immediately. I closed the door to drown out as much noise as possible and sat cross-legged on the bed with my hands pressed together before my chest in the prayer position. In a sonorous voice I slowly repeated *Nam-myo-ho-ren-ge-kyo.* I thought, "Brain! Don't you control the development of cells? Immune system! Do you not work harmoniously for the greater life? I want to leave this hospital in two days. Release your great powers and boost the immune system! I must leave the hospital! I want to go home! I must show actual proof!"

Myo was my head, *Ho* was my throat, *Ren* was my chest, *Ge* was my stomach, and *Kyo* was my legs and extremities. The whole issue was cause and effect. The Mystic Law was the ultimate internal cause and my prayer determined the manifest effect. *Renge* is literally translated to mean "lotus flower." The lotus flower is the only flower known in botany to have the bloom and seeds appear simultaneously. Another definition of *Renge* is the Mystic Law of cause and effect. The effect is contained simultaneously within the cause. I kept reminding myself that my recovery was cause and effect . . . cause and effect . . . cause and effect.

Myo split the air like a sharp sword. From my chest emerged glorious, energetic streams of white healing light, surging up my spine to my head; all my cells were saturated with astral energies. It was impossible for any cell to disobey the command of my brain and my true inner spirit.

Ho, quaked my body as my inner eye watched the light flow grow brighter. In each cell the healing light was vibrantly living. Revitalization took place everywhere cells traveled through my bloodstream and lymph system. Every cell in my body was being touched and renewed with dynamic, mystic energy.

Ren unfolded brilliantly in my chest like a magnificent blue lotus flower in full bloom. I imagined the aura encompassing my karma storehouse and amala consciousness as a transparent egg of golden light. I could see the soot-like stains on the egg, indicating bad karma to be erased. I imagined the light of my enlightened nature burning the spots off with lasers of spectral light, while the healing light flowing throughout my body further cleansed the stains with relentless energy.

Ge was a great chamber in my abdomen, fully accepting the radiant, healing light. All my organs came into focus and I emotionally thanked them. Possessed of their own distinct consciousness, they hailed the greater life victoriously. I focused the light to my spleen, which warehoused and processed blood products. "Spleen!" I shouted internally, "You are healed! Congratulations!

Now join us and fulfill your great functions like never before!" Echoing in my mind was the concept cause and effect . . . cause and effect . . . cause and effect.

Kyo brought the whole visualization into focus as it filled out my arms and legs all the way to the surface of the skin. Energy leapt from my physical body like rising flames lapping the air. The mighty sound of *Kyo* reverberated from my hospital bed beyond the North Star. I knew that one day in the future, I would remember this moment and teach others to empower themselves from the inside out. I was determined to produce a positive result and go home.

With my door closed, I spent one hour in the morning and one hour in the evening performing my mantra-powered visualization. The next morning a phlebotomist came to draw my blood as they did every day. I continued my active visualization of healthy blood cells proliferating in my body. Three o'clock came around and I still didn't have the results from the lab. The nursing station manager had befriended me and called the results up from the computer. She looked at me with that "try, try again" look.

I had expected results too quickly, like some kind of miracle. That was not common sense. I shouldn't expect instant results, but the best results in the most natural manner. I made the determination that tomorrow would be that day. I had told Dr. B. "two days," and that's what it would be. Returning to my room I felt like a determined boxer going to his corner for round two. Somehow I had to show actual proof.

Early that evening I was visited my Mr. M., a Japanese friend and confidant. I told him that I had experienced death, but couldn't explain it yet. In a most encouraging way Mr. M. related the story of Shijo Kingo and his infant daughter Kyo-o. Shijo Kingo was a samurai warrior and physician who lived in 13th-century Japan. He had been a disciple of Nichiren for many years. Late in Shijo Kingo's life, his wife Nichigen-nyo gave birth to a daughter. The child was sickly and not expected to survive. Even as a physician, Shijo Kingo could not cure his baby. Nichiren sent a letter to Shijo Kingo with the following words of encouragement:

> But your faith alone will determine all these things. A sword is useless in the hands of a coward. The mighty sword of the *Lotus Sutra* must be wielded by one coura-geous in faith. Then one will be as strong as a demon armed with an iron staff. I, Nichiren, have inscribed my life in sumi ink, so believe in the Gohonzon with your whole heart. The Buddha's will is the *Lotus Sutra*, but the soul of Nichiren is nothing other than *Nam-myoho-renge-kyo*.[2]

The result of that guidance was a renewed determination by the parents to use the Mystic Law for the sake of their daughter, who then quickly recovered. Although the story of Shijo Kingo and his daughter is more than 700 years old, and took place in a country on the other side of the world, the lesson is timeless. Strong determination in faith, like a lioness on the hunt, and chanting could revitalize my life too. Nothing is more moving than a parent trying to save his or her child. Resolving his doubts, Shijo Kingo showed actual proof in a life-and-death sit-

---

[2] Nichiren Daishonin, "Reply to Kyo-o," in *The Writings of Nichiren Daishonin* (Tokyo: Soka Gakkai, 1999), p. 412.

uation. I had to return to my normal daily life and teach others how to win in their battle with illness.

Mr. M. clearly pointed out that I must believe with my whole heart and take powerful action. His encouragement at that crucial moment filled me with immense resolve. It is said that encouragement can cause people to achieve the impossible, while discouraging words can break a person's confidence and cause their ruin. With the encouragement of Mr. M. in my heart, I readied myself for that evening's crucial battle.

I waited until midnight, when few distracting sounds could interfere. Putting all my anatomical regions on notice, I spent the next hour performing highly focused visualization that centered on dynamic energy in my blood cells. When I finished, my heart felt as bright and clear as a brilliant Barley Moon. I rose an hour before my seven o'clock blood test and repeated the imagery. That day, I reminded the doctors caring for me that if my blood counts were normal, I could go home. They all agreed but were quite skeptical.

The test results were unbelievably slow on Saturday, and my regular attending physician had gone home. When the results came, the doctor in charge for the evening looked them over and handed it to the other doctor of his team. They weren't privy to my determination with Dr. B. nor were they very familiar with my case.

"You are free to go Mr. Atkins, we'll have the staff write up your papers, and I will sign them." I asked them, "What are my blood counts? How good are they?" Glancing back at the numbers on the printout he said, "These counts are good. Your CBC is a little low, but not enough to keep you here any longer. Platelets are good. The others are fine. Go home, Mr. Atkins."

I thanked them, and called Lynn to come pick me up. After I packed, I hounded the ward's desk nurse to expedite my discharge papers. I vowed to never be hospitalized for cancer again! It was now time to go home and face the IRS and bankruptcy court.

EVER VICTORIOUS

Once I got home, I had to prepare myself for another battle familiar to many people stricken by catastrophic illness. When my business creditors found out that I might be terminally ill, many called in their loans, which forced us into bankruptcy. Our business was saved, but our credit was destroyed. From then on, we would have to take care of all operational expenses and purchase all supplies with cash. It seemed like an impossible task.

The Internal Revenue Service had humiliated us by seizing our bank account twice, causing us to bounce checks all over town. We were living under the threat of immediate seizure of all our possessions. We didn't want the pity of the IRS, just some understanding and a little respect. We were willing to enter into a repayment program that we could afford. The IRS negotiated a repayment plan with us, but not without threatening us with swift seizure if we dared miss a payment. The woman who handled our case said she would send the federal marshals right away if I missed one payment. Out of necessity, my daughter had accompanied me to the IRS office for the review. She was so shaken by the woman's nastiness that when she got home, she put sticky notes on her dolls saying, "Please don't take this."

By the time our bankruptcy court appearance came up, I had finished the fifth cycle of chemotherapy and had just taken my second-to-last treatment. I was so wobbly-legged and physically beaten, I could hardly sit through the process. Our request was granted with no complications. Now that the IRS had been temporarily appeased and we had a fresh start with our personal finances and business, I could concentrate on the final cycle of chemotherapy.

I had been randomized in my clinical trial and was scheduled for radiation therapy. The combination of chemotherapy and radiation was being proven to be the best approach in fighting advanced Hodgkin's lymphoma. Unfortunately it meant another assault on my already weakened body and three more months of treatments to endure. As bad as our situation was, I thought about how terrible the situation was for so many other patients and their families. At least I had managed to survive this far and had experienced a remission.

Radiation treatment was like a walk in the park compared to chemotherapy. I was scheduled for 21 treatments to be spread out over a couple of months. I would be receiving upper mantle and lower "Y" cobalt radiation treatments from the bridge of my nose to my groin. The first series of treatments put an extra dose of radiation at my spine and my spleen, which made me violently ill about 45 minutes later. It was a small price to pay for the benefits to be derived. By the time I was going for my radiation treatments, my visualization technique was so precise that I could create a scenario for and effectuate relief from nausea and pain, and could send waves of healing through my body on command.

However, the intense nature of radiation therapy was formidable even with my "secret weapon." After the first series of 11 treatments, I became profoundly exhausted. I could barely raise my voice to chant. The head of the radiotherapy department gave me permission to rest for two weeks and told me to stay away from crowds to avoid infectious diseases. I could do little but sleep and read. The radiation affected my appetite and my weight dropped by 25 pounds. The prednisone steroid I had been taking for chemotherapy had turned me into a maniac with food. My weight varied by 20 pounds a month between the prednisone cycle and the anorexia cycle produced by some of the chemotherapy drugs. Now that I had started radiation, I was once again plagued by loss of appetite and other dehydrating conditions.

It took me three weeks to regain the strength to begin the final ten treatments. My use of visualization for those three weeks had become the silent version, using my inner voice. I was too weak and tired to sit up or use my voice much. It was the worst I had felt since cancer's onset and the barbed path of chemotherapy.

It was a considerable struggle, but by the time I was ready for the second set of treatments, my blood counts had rebounded tremendously, and for the first time in seven months, I felt great. My energy level increased to the point that I felt like I was 25 years old again. Except for perpetually tingling hands and feet, I felt like I did before the onset of cancer. Feeling normal was no small event. Cancer and other serious diseases rob a person of security and cause physical and psychological devastation.

I was reminded of a passage from Nichiren's writings that had provided immense comfort to people suffering from the various difficulties of life: "Winter . . . never fails to turn into spring." My life had been in a state of winter for seven months. My great hope was for life to once again flourish as in the metamorphosis of spring. Our family could barely put food on the table. We could find no government or community agency that could provide relief. Our emergence from the ashes of our struggle could only be accomplished by the power of the human spirit to greet adversity with determination and change weakness into strength. I found that when a human being is put to the test, he or she will fight valiantly or quickly submit to defeat. When a person faithfully uses the Mystic Law, he or she is ever victorious, even when defeat looks inevitable.

In the strict sense of simultaneous cause and effect created through use of the Mystic Law, winter *is* spring. It is on the severe battlefield of life during the present moment where the greatest value can be achieved. By squarely facing impossible obstacles and the reality of your own karma, it is possible to change your destiny and elevate your life condition. The great mantra was the only sword I had the strength to pick up and use.

Proceeding with all of my treatments, I had so much enthusiasm and vitality that people began to ask me what my secret was. Winter had given way and from deep within my life, spring was now slowly emerging. With an ever-victorious attitude, I focused on keeping my body and mind perfectly attuned and experiencing a complete recovery from the effects of treatment. I was attentive to the warning that the toxic nature of chemotherapy could produce more deadly cancers than the one I had survived. With radiation therapy increasing my chances of developing leukemia by 10 percent, I prepared myself for the battle ahead.

After the completion of my treatment, I was required to have a complete physical examination and assorted x-rays every week for the first three months. The type of cancer I had could recur without warning, which would require another round of treatment. For cancer patients, the survival rate is typically measured at the five-year point. If no recurrence has been detected, the long-term survival rate looks good. With Hodgkin's disease, the timetable for possible recurrence is most likely within two years, although it might appear at any time later.

Determined to completely break the chains of karmic illness that had turned my life upside down, I utilized mantra-powered visualization with precise regularity. Not a day went by that I didn't make time to travel throughout my body and congratulate its components for working so perfectly. As the months went by, others who had heard of my apparently successful battle began contacting me. Each person was either ill themselves, or had a loved one who was facing a health crisis.

My benevolence and altruism were tested, because I wanted to forget about cancer. I didn't want to be known as a "one-dimensional person" with his one major accomplishment in life being a cancer survivor. Fifty percent of the people diagnosed with cancer are now surviving for five years. My selfishness and reluctance to talk about my experience in detail was shattered six short months after the end of my treatments.

A close friend of our family who was in her early sixties was diagnosed with a malignant tumor on her upper spine. She was a middle-aged German native who knew of the healing power of Buddhism, but didn't know what to do in her situation. I wrote her a very long letter describing in great detail what I had experienced and how to use mantra-powered visualization.

A few days later, my wife and I visited her in the hospital. Her whole attitude had changed. She was so impressed with the simplicity of the visualization technique and the difference she felt both mentally and physically, that she was in tears. Two days later, she underwent surgery for removal of the tumor. Not only was the operation a success, she was back on her feet and returned to work far ahead of her doctor's expectations. Her cancer never returned.

The amazing aspect of her recovery was her attitude. By using mantra-powered visualization, she was able to directly focus on her tumor to promote healing. Her scenario was to shoot deadly rays into the tumor so when the doctor cut it out it would already be dead.

When I again witnessed the lightning-like power that is produced by this type of imagery, I was ashamed at my petty attitude. What is the purpose of life? If my survival from cancer and death were without reason, then what was my mission? The answer was to lead others toward health and show them how to relieve their suffering. In no way was I some special person who had miraculously overcome cancer with the wave of a wand. My destiny required that I endure the harshest circumstances both mentally and physically. As a mere mortal of meager virtue, small learning, and prone to doubt, I was a good example of an average person who had achieved something great through prayer.

All was not a blissful victory parade for those two years after my complete remission. Rebuilding my business from bankruptcy proved to be a difficult and slow process. Unable to get credit anywhere once the fact of my former insolvency and high risk for cancer recurrence became known, my family and I were forced to live a below-poverty-level existence from week to week.

Neither your material acquisitions nor your status should be the measure of your quality of life. It should be measured by what you overcome. Fighting cancer appears to be a win-or-lose situation. Life cannot be judged in a superficial way. What appears on the surface to be disaster can be turned into great benefit. What looks like a stroke of good fortune can turn into a cause for unhappiness.

I knew that my loved ones and friends sought to ascribe my problems to something. Some of them saw my belief and practice of an Eastern religion as a prime target for their blame. Whenever remarks that disparaged my beliefs came up, I would explain that it wasn't my religious belief but my destiny. I believed that if it hadn't been for chanting, I would be dead. However, trying to convince these people was like talking into outer space and hoping someone would hear me. Staying healthy and crawling out of the financial abyss was the kind of actual proof I needed to show the people who denied the strength of my faith. I needed to take a lot of small steps toward my goal.

I am again reminded of Mrs. E., my Japanese woman friend. I had known her for quite some time and she had the reputation of being very difficult and strict regarding obstacles in general. It didn't matter whether a person was strong or weak, she had the ability to find the sore spot and press it. It had been less than a year since my remission when she asked me when I would write about my experience for submission to our weekly Buddhist newspaper, the *World Tribune*. When I told her that no one would publish the experience of a cancer survivor unless they made it five years, she became very angry with me and said, "You don't really believe you have overcome cancer yet, do you?" I tried to justify my statement from a purely logical viewpoint, but she would have none of it. "Whether you overcome cancer or not isn't the point," she said. "It's your struggle and personal victory people want to know about."

Breaking the chains of karma is difficult, just as tearing down a thick cement wall with a claw hammer is difficult. Karma cannot be seen, only experienced. What kind of causes produces what kind of effects is not an easy thing to determine.

Unchaining the heart and mind from the demons of doubt and continual opposition is the key to realizing a state of absolute freedom. It takes wave after wave from the ocean to smooth down rocks on the beach. Chanting *Nam-myoho-renge-kyo* is like the mighty crashing waves of the ocean and our karma like rocks on a beach. Over a period of time they polish the jagged edges and make them perfectly smooth.

The goal is not to live a life without obstacles and challenges; it is to live a life of absolute freedom by being able to convert any hardship into victory, and all adversity into strength. Just as physical resistance builds muscle, problems toughen you.

Two years passed, then five years. My doctors were totally impressed with my recovery. Unless another doctor saw the scars on my feet from the lymphangiogram or the small blue tattoos that were applied during radiation treatment, it would be impossible to tell that I had ever had cancer. My blood counts were as normal as those of any other healthy person. Except for a few minor complaints about the long-term effects of chemotherapy such as tingling in my feet, I was as good as new.

SHARING

Time has now added some perspective to my experience and my role in the healing arts. My journey was most difficult at first, with one obstacle after another rising up to challenge me. While on that path, I had the opportunity to steer many others away from hopelessness and fear, helping them to become empowered for their difficult battles.

Ironically, many people who might benefit the most from using these techniques are fixed in their attitudes or have already given up. A situation comes to mind about a troubling call I received from a woman who had read my experience in a local newspaper. She queried, cajoled, and bargained with me as if she were shopping for knick-knacks at a local flea market. After I spoke many impassioned words in praise of the techniques of mantra-powered visualization and other people's success with it, the woman finally came clean with her situation.

She said that she had ovarian cancer that had spread. She was in her early 30s, with two small children, and her prognosis was very bad. She argued with me that to do this kind of visualization a person would need special powers of concentration. She repeated her need to find someone who could teach her visualization, and demanded to know what I charged to teach people. When I told her that there was no charge, she became more suspicious than ever. Next, she asked me if I could teach her the technique without the mantra. When I said that the mantra is the key to the technique, she argued that a local Chinese qigong healing society didn't use mantras. Using a mantra was just too strange for her.

After we argued back and forth about whether or not what I promoted actually worked, she said that she might call back if she was interested. I never found out what happened to that woman, but her attitude and harsh words left a permanent impression on me. As much as I would like to help everyone, some people are their own worst enemies. Unable to distinguish between the shallow and the profound, they cannot change. More properly, they will not change. They are rigid, like huge granite stones, and sink to the bottom. If by some chance they could open their heart and minds, even if they were rigid and heavy like large boulders, they could be floated iike pebbles on the great ship of *Nam-myoho-renge-kyo.*

What I discovered with this type of meditative healing is that anyone who earnestly tries their best receives results that are ultimately beneficial. The only exceptions are those who give in to the subjective voices of their own weakness and stop trying. Even if results are not obvious, it is crucial to fight to the end. With *Nam-myoho-renge-kyo* those who fight to the end are victorious, even in death.

My story is only one among many heroic sagas of fighting chronic illness with Buddhist meditation. Freshly inspired by those who are now using it in their own battle, I am intent on making this knowledge available to the public as my life's work. Out of gratitude for the benefits I have received, I will spare no effort in teaching others to the best of my ability for as long as I can.

Glossary

Alaya-vijnana or alaya consciousness: Eighth level of consciousness expounded in Buddhism that corresponds to C. G. Jung's collective unconscious. Also called "storehouse consciousness" or "karma repository." The eighth level of consciousness is located below the realm of conscious awareness. All actions, sensory input, and life experiences that take place through the first seven levels of consciousness are accumulated as karma in this alaya consciousness, which at the same time exerts influence on the working of the other seven consciousnesses. These karmic imprints and potentials are the sphere of consciousness that transmigrates with the amala-vijnana (*see below*) through the cycles of birth and death.

Amala-vijnana or amala consciousness: Below the alaya storehouse consciousness. The basis of spiritual functions, remaining free of all karmic impurity, and identified with the true entity of life, *Nam-myoho-renge-kyo.*

Amrita: Nectar or tears of the Vedic gods.

Ayurveda: Sanskrit term for "life knowledge." Ayurveda is a system of healing developed in India and has more than 5000 years of spiritual acumen and practical application.

Buddha: One who perceives the true nature of all life and leads others to attain the same enlightenment. The Buddha nature exists in all beings and is characterized by the qualities of wisdom, courage, compassion, and life force. In this book, the term "Buddha" refers to either Shakyamuni, Nichiren, or the fundamental enlightenment within all life and people.

Chakra: Life energy centers of the body. See "Kundalini" for more detail.

Chi: Chinese term for the vital life force.

Dharma(s): The law(s) and teaching(s) of the Buddha. The norms of conduct conducive to the accumulation of good karma.

Doshas: Ayurveda teaches that the cycles of life governing human beings are expressed by three major types, or doshas: kapha (water), pitta (fire), and vata (air). From my perspective, the three doshas can be understood as expressions of the unifying quantum law of *Nam-myoho-renge-kyo*.

Expedient Means: Title of the second chapter of the *Lotus Sutra*. "Expedient means" indicates all the sutras, practices, austerities, provisional teachings, and dharma(s) that preceded the revelation of the One Great Vehicle expounded in the *Lotus Sutra*.

Faith factor: Term used by Herbert Benson, M.D., to identify immune system response to the act of faith.

Four Sufferings: Birth, old age, sickness, and death. From other perspectives, this process is also identified as appearance, development, decline, and extinction. This principle can be applied to all manifestations of life, society, the microcosm, the quantum world, and the macrocosm of the universe.

Gohonzon: The embodiment of the law of *Nam-myoho-renge-kyo* and the life of Nichiren Daishonin in the form of a scroll or mandala, which SGI members enshrine in their homes. *Go* means "worthy of honor" and *honzon* means "object of fundamental respect."

Gosho Zenshu: The individual and collected writings of Nichiren Daishonin. *Sho* means "writing(s)" and *go* is an honorific prefix. Nikko Shonin, the Daishonin's immediate successor, used the word *Gosho* in reference to the Daishonin's works and made extraordinary efforts to collect, copy and preserve his teacher's writings. Because of his efforts, most of the Daishonin's important writings have been preserved and transmitted up until today. The collected Gosho includes doctrinal treatises, recorded oral teachings, letters of remonstration, graphs, letters to disciples and lay followers, and so forth. More than 700 of the Daishonin's writings, including copies and fragments, remain today.

Guided Imagery: A meditation technique that is being taught to cancer patients and chronically ill people. They are guided by another person or a recording of a person (or of their own voice) reciting a script that helps them to look inside their body and imagine healing forces coming to their aid. People use specific mental images, prayers, and willpower to achieve a relaxation response. Guided imagery tapes can be found in self-help sections of book stores, and are useful for all sorts of problems, from quitting smoking to simply learning how to relax.

Daisaku Ikeda (1928–): Third president of the Soka Gakkai. Mr. Ikeda is a Buddhist master, founder of Soka University and the acclaimed Soka Schools, the Min-On Concert Association, the Institute of Oriental Philosophy, and the Fuji Art Museum. Mr. Ikeda has received numerous awards and honorary degrees from institutions and universities around the world, including the United Nations Peace Award. Mr. Ikeda is a prolific writer whose many works have been translated into more than a dozen languages.

Karma: Sanskrit word meaning "action." The life tendency or destiny each individual creates through thoughts, words and deeds that exert an often unseen influence over one's future.

Ku: a nonlocal state of existence and non-existence. The mind itself might be said to be a state of ku in that it exists, but is at the same time non-substantial.

Kundalini: "Uncoiling the serpent." Teaching that embraces the principle of seven *chakras* or life energy conduits and spiritual energy centers residing in a human's subtle body. These seven energy centers derive from Hinduism and Tantric Buddhism. The seven major chakras are:

1. *Muladhara* chakra at the base of the spine;

2. *Svadhisthana* chakra at the level of the genitals;

3. *Manipura* chakra at the level of the naval;

4. *Anahata* chakra at the level of the heart;

5. *Visuddha* chakra centered in the throat;

6. *Ajna* chakra between the eyebrows;

7. *Sahasrara* chakra, beyond all duality, and located at the top of the head.

Life dynamic: The true entity of life, *Nam-myoho-renge-kyo.*

Lotus Sutra: The highest teaching of Shakyamuni Buddha, which he taught during the last eight years of his life. The *Lotus Sutra* reveals that all people can attain enlightenment and declares that the Buddha's former teachings should be regarded as preparatory. Reciting excerpts from the *Lotus Sutra* (portions of the second and sixteenth chapters) is part of SGI members' daily Buddhist practice.

Mahayana: One of the two major schools of Buddhism, along with Theraveda (teachings of the elders). Mahayana Buddhism has taken root and flourished in Nepal, China, Korea, Japan, and now the Western world. Mahayana can be divided into two branches: The *Lotus Sutra* that revealed Shakyamuni's enlightenment and earlier teachings that increase people's capacity to understand the Buddha's ultimate teaching embodied in the *Lotus Sutra*. In general, Mahayana Buddhism promotes the idea that all people are fundamentally Buddhas, that earthly desires cannot be completely eliminated—only elevated—and that Buddhism should not be kept to oneself, but instead should be spread to all corners of the world.

Maio-lo (711–782): Restorer of T'ien-T'ai (Tendai) Buddhism.

Maka Shikan or *Great Concentration and Insight*: One of the Great Teacher T'ien-t'ai's three major works, along with the *Hokke Gengi*, and *Hokke Mongu*.

Mandala: The term *mandala* originally meant a round or square altar on which Buddhas are placed. It is translated in China by terms meaning "perfectly endowed" or "cluster of blessings." The mandala in Nichiren Daishonin's Buddhism is the Gohonzon.

Manos-vijnana or manos consciousness: The seventh of the Nine Levels of Consciousness. The nine levels are defined as smell, touch, taste, sound, sight, the conscious mind, the unconscious, the karma repository, and fundamental enlightenment. The Sanskrit word *manas*, from which *manos* is derived, means "to ponder." This consciousness performs the function of abstract thought and discerns the inner world. Awareness of the self is said to originate at this level. The passionate attachment to ego, which functions to create negative karma, is also regarded as the working of the manos consciousness, influenced by the eighth level, or alaya consciousness.

Mantra: Sanskrit word meaning "True Words." A "formula" consisting of esoteric words or syllables, which are said to embody mystic powers and were used originally in Brahmanism. Esoteric Buddhism views mantras as distillations of Buddhist truth. Mantras are often employed in rituals in which they are said to help achieve union with a metaphorical Buddha known as Dainichi (Tathagata Mahavirochana).

Mantra-powered visualization: The meditation technique first expounded upon by Soka Gakkai Vice President, Takehisa Tsuji, which involves using faith and the mantra *Nam-myoho-renge-kyo* along with one's imagination for the purpose of healing.

Mindfulness meditation: A method of dhyana meditation used to achieve higher states of consciousness, now being used as a relaxation tool in alternative medicine.

Mudras: Signs and gestures made with the hands and fingers, which symbolize the enlightenment and vows of the Buddhas and Bodhisattvas. Mudras are commonly employed in the esoteric Shingon form of Buddhism as a way of achieving union with the metaphorical Buddha, Mahavirochana (Dainichi).

Mystic Law: *Nam-myoho-renge-kyo.*

Nam-myoho-renge-kyo: The fundamental component of the

practice of Nichiren Daishonin's Buddhism, it expresses the true entity of life that allows each individual to directly tap his or her enlightened nature. Although the deepest meaning of *Nam-myoho-renge-kyo* is revealed only through its invocation, the literal meaning is: *Nam* (devotion), the fusion of one's life with the universal; *myoho* (Mystic Law), the entity of the universe and its phenomenal manifestations; *renge* (lotus), the simultaneity of cause and effect; *kyo* (Buddha's teaching), all phenomena and activities of life. *Myoho-renge-kyo* is the title of the twenty-eight chapters of the *Lotus Sutra* translated by Kumarajiva (344–413).

Nichiren Daishonin (1222–1282): The founder of the school of Buddhism upon which the Soka Gakkai International (*see*) bases its activities. He inscribed the true object of worship for the observation of one's mind, the Gohonzon, and established the invocation of *Nam-myoho-renge-kyo* as the universal practice to attain enlightenment.

Nichiren Shoshu: Literally, the "orthodox Nichiren sect," which regards Nichiren as its founder and Nikko Shonin as his successor, with a head temple in Taiseki-ji in Shizuoka Prefecture, Japan. Nichiren Shoshu was formerly allied with the lay organization, Soka Gakkai, until 1990, when it excommunicated all 10 million members of the lay organization because the latter insisted on reformation of the priesthood and that the Nichiren Shoshu open up to modernization.

Nirvana: Enlightenment, the ultimate goal of Buddhist practice. An awakening to the true nature of all phenomena. The word actually means "blown out," and is variously translated as extinction, emancipation, cessation, quiescence, or non-rebirth. Nirvana was originally regarded as the state in which all illusions and desires and the cycle of birth and death itself are extinguished. From the standpoint of Nichiren Daishonin's Buddhism, nirvana is an attainable life condition existing in this world and reality. Nirvana is a life-state of Buddhahood that is impervious to birth and death, rather than the idea of an eternal heaven.

One Great Vehicle: The law of *Myoho-renge-kyo* expounded in the *Lotus Sutra.*

Pali Canon: Oldest of the known Buddhist texts.

Paramita (Six Paramitas): Practices that Mahayana Bodhisattvas undertake to attain enlightenment. Generally, *paramita* is a Sanskrit term interpreted as "perfection" or "having reached the opposite shore." The six paramitas are: almsgiving; keeping the precepts; forbearance; assiduousness; meditation; obtaining wisdom which enables one to perceive the true nature of all things.

Prana: "Wind" or "vital force." Sanskrit term from the Upanisads that represents "the center." A simile of Brahmanism indicating that prana is representative of an immanent, intra-cosmic force. Life force.

Pre-*Lotus Sutra* Teachings: Teachings Shakyamuni expounded before the Lotus Sutra. According to T'ien-t'ai's classification of the Buddha's teachings into five periods, in the order in which they were taught, the teachings of the Kegon, Agon, Hodo, and Hannya periods constitute the pre-*Lotus Sutra* teachings.

Qigong: Chinese health and wellness practice derived from Taoism.

Quantum world view: A perception similar to the Buddhist idea of dependent origination. Quantum consciousness recognizes all life as a stream of intelligent energy.

Relaxation response: A term used by Harvard professor, Herbert Benson, M.D., for the scientifically measurable influence of faith and prayer in healing, detailed in his book, *The Relaxation Response*.

Remembered wellness: Term used by Herbert Benson to refer to a person's immune response produced by remembering a state of wellness.

Shakyamuni: Also known as Siddartha or Gautama. Born in Nepal about 2500 years ago, he was the first recorded Buddha and founder of Buddhism. For 50 years he taught various sutras (teachings) culminating in the *Lotus Sutra*, which he declared to be his ultimate teaching.

Shiki-shin-funi: Principle of the oneness of body and mind.

Siddhartha or Gautama: Birth names of Shakyamuni Buddha.

Simonton Method: A visualization technique devised in the early 1970s by radiation oncologist Dr. Carl Simonton and his wife, Stephanie Matthews-Simonton, a psychologist. The patient pictures immune system cells as numerous and strong, and cancer cells as isolated and weak.

Soka Gakkai International (SGI): The worldwide organization of Nichiren Daishonin's Buddhism, led by President Daisaku Ikeda, active in 183 nations and territories, and devoted to the creation of values through the promotion of peace, culture, and education. The United States branch of this Buddhism is called the SGI-USA.

Superluminal: Faster-than-light phenomena in quantum theory. Relevant non-local concept explored by Nick Herbert in his book *Faster than Light: Superluminal Loopholes in Physics* (p. 15).

Ten Worlds/Three Thousand Worlds: There are Ten Worlds that are part of a larger schematic called the Three Thousand Worlds (*Ichinen Sanzen*, or 3000 Worlds in a single life moment). They are conditions of life, or worlds within human consciousness, that are ever present and inherent in all life. The Ten Worlds are Hell, Hunger, Animality, Anger, Humanity, Heaven, Learning, Realization, Bodhisattva (altruism), and Buddhahood (enlightenment). Each one of the Ten Worlds has an identical Ten Worlds within it, like bubbles within a bubble, equaling 100 potential worlds. This is known as the "mutual possession." For example, if I am suffering terribly because of a tragic event, I would be in the state of Hell, but in that hell is the potential of all other Ten Worlds. I then chant daimoku and immediately bring out the Tenth World of Buddhahood. My life condition is then raised and I might realize the true cause of my suffering. I am then in the state of Learning or Realization. My suffering, although not forgotten, might rise to the world of Heaven (sometimes referred to as Rapture), where the dominant world of Hell could be reversed; Heaven would then become the dominant world and Hell its mutually possessed world. These Ten Worlds fall into and are influenced by the Ten Factors, which are the dynamic of all life. These factors are Appearance, Nature, Entity, Power, Influence, Internal Cause, Relation, Latent Effect, Manifest Effect, and their Consistency from beginning to end. Multiplying the 100 worlds by the Ten Factors produces 1000 potential worlds. These 1000 worlds are influenced by the Three Realms that characterize all life. The Three Realms are: the realm of the environment; the realm of living beings; the realm of the five components of form, perception, conception, volition, and consciousness. The 1000 worlds multiplied by the Three Realms equals 3000 worlds. All things that live, from an amoeba to an extraterrestrial, contain these 3000 worlds.

Three Vehicles: The men and women described in the *Lotus Sutra* as Learners, Adepts, and Bodhisattvas—or those of Learning, Realization, and Bodhisattva.

T'ien-t'ai or Chih-i: Synonymous with the Tendai (sect). School of Northern Mahayana Buddhism founded by Chih-i, who is commonly referred to as the Great Teacher T'ien-t'ai. He organized Buddhism into five periods and asserted that Shakyamuni's ultimate teaching was found in the *Lotus Sutra*.

Toda, Josei: Second President of the Soka Gakkai.

Yoga: Applies to all the disciplines and philosophies originating in India. A form of meditation developed in ancient India, aimed at liberating one from the physical limitations of the body, or, more broadly, from sufferings, by achieving concentration of mind and fusing with truth. There are several schools of yoga that employ a variety of disciplines, including breath control, special postures, etc. Today some of the physical yogic disciplines are widely practiced for health and tranquility of mind, without any particular religious motivation.

Bibliography

Benson, M.D., Herbert with Marge Stark. *Timeless Healing: The Power and Biology of Belief.* New York: Scribner, 1996.

Camp, John Michael Francis. *Magic, Myth & Medicine.* New York: Taplinger, 1974.

Chopra, Deepak. *Quantum Healing: Exploring the Frontiers of Mind/Body Medicine.* New York: Bantam, 1990.

Cousins, Norman. *Head First: The Biology of Hope and the Healing Power of the Human Spirit.* New York: Dutton, 1989.

Dossey, M.D., Larry. *Healing Words: The Power of Prayer and the Practice of Medicine.* San Francisco: Harper-SanFrancisco, 1993.

Eadie, Betty, Curtis Taylor (contributor) and Melvin Morse. *Embraced by the Light.* New York: Bantam, 1994.

Goleman, Daniel and Joel Gurin, eds. *Mind Body Medicine: How to Use Your Mind for Better Health.* Yonkers, NY: Consumer Reports Books, 1993.

Herbert, Nick. *Faster than Light: Superluminal Loopholes in Physics.* New York: Dutton, 1989.

Ikeda, Daisaku. "The One Essential Phrase Part 2." *World Tribune,* June 7, 1996.

Nichiren Daishonin. *Gosho Zenshu.* Tokyo: Soka Gakkai, 1952.

———. *The Writings of Nichiren Daishonin.* The Gosho Translation Committee. Tokyo: Soka Gakkai, 1999.

Pearsall, Paul. *Superimmunity: Master Your Emotions and Improve Your Health.* Boston: McGraw-Hill, 1987.

Rossman, Martin. *Healing Yourself: A Step-by-Step Program for Better Health through Imagery.* New York: Walker & Co., 1987.

Siegel, M.D., Bernie. *Love, Medicine & Miracles: Lessons Learned About Self-Healing from a Surgeon's Experience with Exceptional Patients.* New York: Harper & Row, 1986.

Tsuji, Takehisa. "Buddhism and Medicine," *Seikyo Times,* no. 206.

———. "The Key to Revitalization," *Seikyo Times,* no. 243.

Watson, Burton, tr. *The Lotus Sutra.* New York: Columbia University Press, 1993.

Index

Photo by Inga Mucha

ABOUT THE AUTHOR

CHARLES ATKINS studied and practiced magick, divination, and Eastern religions in the 60s and 70s, then began practicing Nichiren Buddhism in 1974 with the Soka Gakkai. He has been a professional freelance writer on mysticism, healing, and business since 1970.